Praise for ARC Le

"One of the most thought-provoking books I've ever read. It touched numerous nerves with me and shone a light beautifully on my own leadership, my years at the BBC, ITV and Disney and the way we lead at Nickelodeon. It's a book shareholders will be waving at CEOs, expecting Authentic, Responsible, Courageous leadership as key to providing a competitive edge. A must-read for any ambitious CEO and for management teams – whether their focus is the bottom line, thriving in the face of 21st-century challenges, or leaving their own personal legacy in the organisation."

Tim Patterson, Vice President, Director of Programming, Nickelodeon

"I found this book unbelievably thought-provoking. It is clearly based on an enormous amount of research, but is incredibly easy to read and is the most engaging management book I've read – almost like reading a novel. Importantly, it raises a number of questions that forced me to challenge myself and my leadership at a fundamental level.

I'd recommend this book to anyone in a leadership position – not just those at the 'top' of organisations, but those in junior and mid-level roles. It's of clear value to our next generation of leaders, but I believe it's the leaders of today that need this book most. Today's business demands that we be more Authentic, Responsible and Courageous now. We can't afford to simply shrug our shoulders, continue with 'business as usual' and hope the better leaders of tomorrow will pick up the pieces."

Tony Cooper, Entrepreneur and wine importer, following ten years as a Partner at Deloitte

"This book has had a real impact on me. I absolutely believe these three ARC qualities are necessary to become a better leader. The more I read, the more I found I wanted to discuss them with others – to deepen our understanding of what these words mean to us and why they resonate so much.

For these reasons and others, I'd recommend this book as the framework for a leadership programme. Business schools in particular would do well to pay attention: given what's gone on in corporations over the years, they need to take

i

greater responsibility for producing future business leaders who aren't simply able to profitably grow a business, but are – to their core – Authentic, Responsible and Courageous."

Karen Lombardo, former Worldwide Head of Human Resources, Gucci Group

"Reading this book is a very intense experience. Everyone who dives into this vast blue hole of carefully interwoven ideas is sure to have a personal experience. The author gets us to smile, to laugh, to be intrigued by the evidence, but there is little relaxation to be found here. Like many books it challenges your thinking. Like few books it challenges your heart. It is unforgettable, unsettling, relentless and life changing. It is a 'keeper', something you put on the shelf and come back to time and time again."

David Cannon, Managing Director, AndersonLaing

"Since my executive coach introduced me to the three ARC qualities, they've become my 'mighty three'. The words 'Authentic, Responsible and Courageous' are on the wall in my office and together they inform every major decision we make at The Grand Appeal."

Nicola Masters, Director, UK children's charity Wallace and Gromit's Grand Appeal

"An excellent book and an inspirational template for a better way of leading and living. It is positive, hopeful, intelligent, friendly, shrewd, eye-opening, evidence-based and incredibly generous. It's a book that challenges and supports us like a great coach or trainer would do, provoking fresh insights and creating a renewed, refreshed sense of purpose – part character review, part campaign for personal overhaul. I will undoubtedly read it a number of times.

This would be a wonderful centrepiece to a leadership development programme, and what an awesome course that could be. Indeed, I predict that this book will become a standard text. It's a book that deserves big success and to establish Richard Boston as an important figure in the world of leadership and personal development."

Phil Hayes, Chairman, Management Futures

"I get more and more out of this book every time I read it. It combines stories, insights, the author's own professional and personal experiences, copious research and thought-provoking questions, which bring the ARC concepts to life and help the reader apply them directly to their own leadership.

The model seems simple at first, but do not be fooled: beneath the surface, in the tensions within and between each of the three ARC qualities, there is a great deal of complexity. If you are serious about making real changes to your leadership, do not just read this book. As tempting as it is to keep reading, I would strongly recommend you spend time on the various questions and exercises it offers."

Rebecca Stevens, whose previous roles include heading up leadership, talent and organisational development at Kimberly-Clark (Australia), Deloitte (UK) and BAT (Global)

"I love this book. I've read it, re-read it, and written notes in all the margins. The author is very generous with his knowledge, and left me sufficiently hooked to find more information online. It's a rigorous, intelligent book that doesn't try to hide its intelligence. It treats us like adults, resisting the temptation to offer quick, superficial tricks and fixes. Instead, it challenges us to make a fundamental shift, to make ourselves better – both as leaders and as people – and feels all the more decent because of it. It's not just a book to read; it's a book to use, to work through (its various exercises are excellent, practical and eye-opening). I'd recommend ARC to anyone who wants to build a career they can be proud of – particularly if they're also keen to be proud of how they did it."

Adam Burns, Editor-in-Chief, MeetTheBoss TV

"ARC brings new insights into what it means to be a great leader. It conveys the important benefits of being yourself, building on your strengths, being responsible for your actions and those of your team and facing the fear of making brave decisions, whilst being able to stand by them.

The book is as absorbing as reading a novel and demonstrates what ARC means through practical exercises that encourage self-awareness and reflection. I am working hard to integrate Authentic, Responsible and Courageous leadership into my daily life as a member of the senior team at the British Library. Doing so is

helping me to develop the trust of my colleagues and stakeholders and ultimately to improve my performance."
Lucie Burgess, Head of Content Strategy, Research and Operations,
The British Library

"ARC has reinforced my compass, the guiding principles that help me navigate a world filled with policies and procedures. The book's proposition is easy to grasp and easy to buy into, and the stories and case studies are interesting and inspiring. More importantly, though, the author brings real tangible clarity to what it means to be Authentic, Responsible and Courageous. So, I've not only enjoyed the book, I've taken away clear actions that will improve my performance both as a leader and as a follower of others. I recommend this book to leaders at all levels, from high level executives to leaders in the making."
Mark Griffiths, Head of Customer Services for North America,
Workplace Systems

"This book is for anyone ready to take on the most fundamental leadership challenge: effectively leading yourself. You don't have to be a "line manager" to benefit from this work, but you do have to be ready to take a good hard look at yourself, act with consciousness and integrity on what you find, and shamelessly stand up for what you believe in. ARC is *the* mantra for our individual and collective longevity."
Britta van Dyk, Senior Consultant, Maximus International, and board member at Moringa Project

● ● ●

AUTHENTIC + RESPONSIBLE + COURAGEOUS®

ARC
LEADERSHIP

**From surviving to
thriving in a complex world**

RICHARD BOSTON

Authentic + Responsible + Courageous
is a registered trademark of Richard Boston

The ARC logo is a trademark of Richard Boston

Cover design: Objective Ingenuity
Production: Alison Rayner

Published by LeaderSpace
Harwood House, 43 Harwood Road, London SW6 4QP
All enquiries to: publications@leader-space.com

First published 2014

ISBN: 978-0-9929445-2-0 (Paperback)
ISBN: 978-0-9929445-1-3 (eBook-ePub)
ISBN: 978-0-9929445-0-6 (eBook-Kindle)

® Feel the Fear and Do It Anyway is the registered trademark of
The Jeffers/Shelmerdine Family Trust
and is used with their permission.

For Jane,
who has been on her own
Authentic, Responsible and Courageous
journey and has helped me on mine.

For Jim, Jon, Mark and Paul,
whose Authentic, Responsible and Courageous lives
have inspired me,
though I imagine they'll be surprised to hear it.

For Evie,
who'll need these three in her toolkit
as she tackles the world of tomorrow.

And for Robin and Jenni,
for all the obvious reasons,
and some far less obvious.

• ● •

About the Author

• ● •

RICHARD BOSTON is a psychologist who coaches leaders and leadership teams across the globe, for household names like Gucci, Heineken, the NHS, Siemens and Shell, as well as SMEs, charities, governments and various nations' armed forces. He is founder and Managing Director of his own consultancy firm, acts as external faculty for select business schools and sometimes partners with other consulting practices. He's also a speaker and mud-runner, and he once won four awards for bravery.

Additional ARC Resources

• ● •

YOU CAN FOLLOW Richard on Twitter at @rejboston or contact him via publications@leader-space.com. You can also join the conversation via the 'ARC: Authentic + Responsible + Courageous' group on LinkedIn and the 'ARC Leadership' page on Facebook.

You can download additional ARC resources at www.leader-space.com/arc-resources, and you'll find related articles on the website's 'Our Thinking' page.

Acknowledgements

• ● •

I'M INCREDIBLY GRATEFUL to everyone who has contributed to the creation of this book. Claire Davey asked me to clarify my coaching philosophy, which triggered a critical epiphany. Professor Peter Hawkins encouraged me from the beginning and our conversations helped shape the book at a conceptual and structural level.

I'm also grateful to those people who sowed some of the seeds that fed the development of ARC as a concept – authors and researchers too numerous to name here but whose work is referenced throughout. Those who stand out most are Harald Harung and his colleagues, for their work on authenticity; Robert Biswas-Diener for his work on courage; Roy Baumeister for his work on willpower; Robert Kegan and Lisa Lahey for the work on immunity to change; Bernard Cooke who first got me thinking about resilience and thus played a key role in the development of the Resilience Bomb; Edelman for their surveys on trust; Professor Andrew Oswald on questions of balance; Professor Manfred Kets de Vries for his generosity and insights. Thanks, too, to the late Susan Jeffers PhD, who sadly passed away while I was writing this book, and to her husband Mark Shelmerdine for approving my use of the phrase 'feel the fear and do it anyway' – far and away the best way to sum up my thoughts on courage.

I'd like to thank the Master Connector, Anton Horne, who opened doors into the British Army that aided my exploration of all three ARC qualities – thanks in no small part to Lieutenant Colonel Charlie Antelme DSO, and to Major Matt Cansdale MBE PARA from the Royal Military Academy at Sandhurst.

I'd also like to thank everyone who has thrown themselves heart and soul into the ARC Leadership programme – whether participants, programme managers, coordinators or fellow facilitators, past and present – including Ro Paddon, Mary Malecaut, Paul Noel, Angela Sherring, Jude O'Neill and Helen Millen, who've been championing the programme across Europe, the Middle East and Africa. Plus Watershed's Stephen Waters and Phil Hayes, Tim Cox and Loubna Laroussi at Management Futures, who were promoting the book and arranging seminars long before it hit the shelves.

A number of people gave early drafts of the book invaluable attention and their feedback was much appreciated. These include many of the people I've already mentioned, as well as Lucie Burgess, Adam Burns, David Cannon, Tony Cooper, Jon Cowell, Bernie Folan, Mark Griffiths, Piers Ibbotson, Tim Patterson, Dr David Pendleton, Denise Purssey, Séverine Rivière, Daryll Scott, Ameet Thakkar and Jo-Ann White. And, then of course, there was the invaluable contribution of my editor Jackie King.

Finally, I'd like to thank the colleagues and clients whose faith in our relationship and endless quest for something better has inspired me to be Courageous in exploring new frontiers. I count myself incredibly lucky in this regard and there are far too many to thank individually, but five names should be highlighted. Their faith, challenge and encouragement were instrumental in getting me to where I am today: Rebecca Stevens, Karen Lombardo and Cheryl Sims-Hancock (who have already read and critiqued the book), and Mark Gallagher and Glen Fox (whose copies are on their way).

● ● ●

Contents

• • •

1

® Feel the Fear and Do It Anyway is the registered trademark of The Jeffers/Shelmerdine Family Trust and is used with their permission.

Preface

Peter Hawkins

Professor of Leadership at Henley Business School

● ● ●

WHEN I WAS YOUNG I thought that privilege and power would bring with them freedom. However, as I got older and took on many roles that involved leadership, I discovered that the privilege and power of leadership brought with it not freedom, but responsibility. I saw the truth in Shakespeare's words "Uneasy lies the head that wears the crown."[1] I felt first-hand the Sufi poet Rumi's observation that "Leadership is a poison" except to the leader who possesses the "antidote" in their heart[2].

So what is that antidote? What is it that will enable us to wear the mantle of leadership with ease?

In my book *The Wise Fools Guide to Leadership*[3], I wrote that leadership is less a role and more an attitude, and that it begins when we stop blaming others or making excuses. I was endeavouring to highlight the awareness that at the heart of leadership lie not competencies that can be acquired, but attitudes of being.

In this valuable guidebook to stepping up to leadership, Richard Boston shows us that there are three central qualities that all leaders need to constantly develop: we need to be Authentic, Responsible and Courageous. Not only does he convincingly argue that we need all three, but also that we need to know how to integrate all three in our daily engagement – not only with those we lead, but with our peers, those we report to and indeed all our many stakeholders. To this list I would add what Abrams calls "the more than human world", the wider environment that sustains all of us and without which there is no life and nothing to lead.

3

We've achieved some great things as a species over the past two thousand years and the pace of change is accelerating on all fronts – technological, social, political and economic. As a species, we have power our ancestors could barely imagine. But, sadly, that power has outgrown our wisdom. And, as a senior official from the United Nations once said, "If the gap between our power and our wisdom is not redressed soon, I do not have much hope for our prospects."[4]

Some of the research and opinion on leadership has tried to bridge this gap. In the past twenty years we've had calls for Authentic Leadership, Transformational Leadership, Ethical Leadership and Fierce Leadership. We've been encouraged to embrace Corporate Social Responsibility and complexity and to stop deifying and demonising individual leaders. All of these approaches have something to offer, but they all seem to focus on one thing at the expense of others.

Never have we more needed guidance on how to take leadership without poisoning ourselves and others. In today's "VUCA" environment (volatile, unpredictable, complex and ambiguous), simple recipes and formulas for leadership are no longer fit for purpose. Which is where this book comes in. Richard Boston argues compellingly that three seemingly simple qualities lie at the core of great leadership: authenticity, responsibility and courage. It's these three ARC qualities that will help us survive and thrive, both as leaders and as a species, in our evolving environment. Not only that, but they offer us something that transcends organisational, national and cultural boundaries.

The book you now hold in your hands aims to bring clarity to those three qualities. It seeks to help you come to terms with what being Authentic, Responsible and Courageous means to you in your leadership context. It'll show you what you, your people and your organisation stand to gain from your attempts to be more Authentic, Responsible and Courageous. And it will help you explore your own personal challenges and how developing these three qualities will help both you and those around you. I constantly paused when reading this book, and found myself prompted to reflect on how am I stepping up to what life is needing from me, rather than doing what comes easily.

Throughout the book, Richard speaks to us in two languages that are familiar to most leaders and two that are not. The first is the language of research and hard evidence, with an impressive list of references and endnotes. The second is the language of stories and personal experiences. As a psychologist, consultant, coach and speaker who has worked closely with over a thousand leaders from a range of organisations and cultures, Richard has plenty of 'war stories' to draw upon. He's also drawn a number of case studies from elsewhere in the leadership literature. But it's not just other leaders' stories we're working with as we read this book: it's our own. Richard asks us repeatedly to enter the most instructive classroom of all: our own life and work as leaders. I'd strongly encourage us all to do as he asks: to examine our own experience and learn from it – whether it's things we have done in the past or the things we are doing in the present. If you do, you'll find reading this book an intense but highly practical and effective use of your time.

Richard writes with a third language, less common in books of this kind: a frank, friendly, good-humoured tone that holds us accountable but doesn't judge us. Anyone who's taken on a leadership role will have noticed the strange psychological effect it has on them. All of a sudden, you're not just 'you' any more; you're also someone else. Richard has chosen to stand alongside us – to understand how hard it can be for us to be consistently Authentic, Responsible and Courageous and to manage the tensions between the three. He offers us questions to ponder, useful guidance and a range of practical tips. He also shares his own personal successes and failures where these three qualities are concerned. But he does not pretend to have all the answers.

The combination of these three 'languages' makes for a compelling read, but there's a fourth that's far more important. Richard has a talent for integrating research, anecdotes and ideas from an eclectic range of sources including psychology and spirituality, martial arts and medicine, business and sports, philosophy and neuroscience, hypnosis and quantum physics. He offers us something that pulls these threads together, but he doesn't tie them all up too neatly. Instead, he draws our attention to the inherent conflicts and paradoxes in the way we think about ourselves and our leadership. In doing so, he's asking us to *really think* as we work through this book – rather than simply soak up what he's saying.

I see in Richard a man on a personal mission to help us all be more Authentic, Responsible and Courageous – both as leaders and in our other roles in life. At the heart of this book, you'll find his humanity, curiosity and passion. "ARC is bigger than the book, and both are bigger than me," he said during one of our conversations about this book. The book itself is clearly born of his own determination to be Authentic, Responsible and Courageous – rather than being an attempt to generate some easily sellable ideas.

This is an important book. The three ARC qualities apply far beyond the world of work, but the focus here is very much on Authentic, Responsible and Courageous *leadership*. I'd recommend it to anyone in or considering a leadership role, and to anyone involved in coaching, mentoring or training the leaders of today and tomorrow. It's not only highly readable, it's a book that will leave you feeling both challenged and understood. It's a book that will leave you inspired to demonstrate these three ARC qualities in your own leadership, and to encourage others to do the same.

Peter Hawkins
March 2014

PART

1

Why and how to read this book

1

The demand for Authentic, Responsible and Courageous leadership

● ● ●

"As the world becomes ever more dangerous and our problems more complex and dire, we long for truly distinguished leaders, men and women who deserve our respect and loyalty... The business media have exposed one scandal after another – criminally greedy CEOs, boards that do little more than rubber-stamp executive whims, companies willing to trade customers' lives for profits, and corrupt and partisan political leaders.**"**

Warren Bennis, leadership pioneer[5]

ASK PEOPLE TO NAME the three qualities they believe are most important in a leader and you'll end up with a very long list. Some words will appear more than others: "intelligence" and "integrity" are pretty common, as are "wisdom", "determination", "focus" and "fairness". They'll be admirable traits that few people would object to their leader possessing. So why have I chosen to focus on these three 'ARC qualities' (pronounced 'arc' rather than 'A.R.C.')?

Three reasons: firstly, I see the combination of these three leadership qualities encompassing or underpinning most others.

Secondly, I've found these three qualities – used together – offer a powerful new way of making leadership decisions. The three together offer so much more than any one alone.

8

Thirdly, but most importantly, the more I've shared, worked with and researched these three qualities, the more convinced I've become that they are critical in leaders and organisations who are hoping to survive and thrive in a world of increasing complexity while trying to turn back a growing tide of mistrust.

We need to do more, faster, with less – and to higher quality. We're required to learn, un-learn and re-learn faster and faster to match the pace of change and outperform the competition. Our staff and stakeholders grow more and more diverse, increasing the chances of conflict between competing priorities. We face increasing scrutiny from customers, end users, shareholders, legislators, regulators, the media and the general public. At the same time, faith in leaders and their organisations is, sadly, in decline. Staff, customers, service users and investors feel their loyalty tested; regulators and legislators seek tighter controls; journalists feel they are guaranteed a continuing run of shocking headlines.

ARC's ability to help us meet these challenges is key to its appeal and makes it relevant whether you're a CEO, middle manager or first time leader, or you're a non-executive board member, shareholder or trustee who wants more from an organisation's leadership team.

Before we look at how exactly ARC can help, though, what exactly *are* the challenges we're facing?

A world of increasing complexity and interdependence

Whether you work in a global organisation or a national institution, a medium-sized business, a school, a charity or a local government agency, you'll have been feeling the significant effects of change. You'll recognise what Professor of Leadership Peter Hawkins calls "the unholy trinity" at every turn: "Do more – quicker, with less and to a higher standard than before"[6]. It's an expectation that affects all of us. And it *will not* get better: people's expectations are *continuing to rise*. More than 79% of people in the so-called 'Developing World'[7] now have mobile phones, the majority of which have internet capability[8]. This means the disparities between the 'haves' and the 'have nots' are becoming more apparent to those who, a few years ago, would have had far less appreciation of what people in the 'Developed World' take for granted. This understandably raises their expectations. Thus demand increases while the supply of raw materials diminishes. In response, some policy makers have suggested reducing populations (or at least population growth) in emerging markets, but this will more likely *increase* people's expectations while at the same time reducing our ability to meet them. People born into smaller families typically have a greater sense of entitlement than those from larger families.

So, the unholy trinity is here to stay. The result is an environment characterised by ambiguity, uncertainty and a feeling of accelerating change. It's a world where becoming successful is far easier than remaining successful.

Ask yourself…[9]

- How is my team or organisation's external environment changing?

- What is happening internally to mirror those changes?

- What gaps does this highlight (in the team or organisation's strategy and culture; its infrastructure, skills and resources; the relationships we have with each other; the relationships we have with stakeholders outside the team/ organisation)?

- What does my team and/or organisation need me to do in order to address these challenges, whether by myself or with the help of others?

> This book is about these questions and others like them. Each time you come across a question, I'd encourage you to take the time to digest it. Spend some time thinking about how it applies to you.

The chances are, your environment is demanding that you...

- Do more, quicker, better, with fewer resources

- Make faster, higher quality decisions

- Be increasingly resilient

- Be more adaptable, in terms of behaviours, attitudes and mind sets

- Manage relationships more efficiently and effectively with increasingly diverse stakeholders, each with their own conflicting priorities

- Manage accountability across matrices and organisational boundaries

- Inspire commitment in an increasingly diverse and transient workforce

If you're leading a company with shareholders, you'll also be facing pressure to deliver increasing profitability (and thus better dividends) without seeming greedy. Contrary to popular belief, your shareholders and the analysts that feed their opinions will be looking at you to perform consistently over time – otherwise they'll desert you. They're also increasingly interested in how your company makes its profits and what it does with them: they want ethical profitability, often with a dash of philanthropy, so they can feel good while they make money.

If you're working at a senior level in an organisation that has trustees or governors, you will be under pressure to use your shrinking resources wisely and sustainably. Most trustees and governors will be paying increased attention to your competence and clarity of vision while demanding greater involvement in key decisions and a greater return on their own investment of time. They'll expect innovative approaches to fundraising and collaboration with other organisations.

If you're a middle manager, you'll be affected by your leaders' reactions to the challenges they're facing at the top, but you'll be experiencing those challenges quite differently – after all, it's you that needs to deliver on the promises they've made to their stakeholders.

You'll also be facing pressure from below, from the 'front line', and you'll probably be trying to work out how to balance a rewarding career with a life outside work.

I'll explain later how the three ARC qualities help us meet these challenges. Before I do, I'd like us to look beyond the world's increasing complexity and interdependence to a third trend that demands leaders be more Authentic, Responsible and Courageous…

The rising tide of mistrust

> "Effective finance and banking devoid of confidence and trust is an anathema – a scenario so impractical as to be beyond recognition. Loss of confidence and trust results in the loss of legitimacy, and when this occurs, commercial activity and business performance do not simply dissipate and decline, they disappear. This is the story of the global financial crisis."
>
> The Henley Manifesto:
> Restoring Confidence and Trust in UK PLC[10]

The more complex and interdependent our lives, organisations, cultures and economies become, the more reliant we are on trust – and the more fragile it becomes. As the political economist John Stuart Mill said in 1848, "The advantage to mankind of being able to trust one another penetrates into every crevice and cranny of human life."[11]

Banks rely on trust when they lend money. For customers to make deposits, essentially lending the banks money, they need to trust the banks, the regulators and their governments to protect their assets. Innovation, too, relies on a degree of trust: consider the millions spent protecting patents by producers of mobile technology.

In hard times, trust acts as a buffer to criticism and bad news: when people trust an organisation they are apparently twice as likely to believe positive messages about it than negative ones; when they *don't* trust an organisation, they're almost four times as likely to believe the negatives[12], and they're less likely to buy and keep shares[13]. Similarly, trust drives business performance by attracting endorsements, reducing marketing costs and enabling organisations to opt for premium pricing[14].

Trust is equally important *within* organisations as it's increasingly difficult to monitor people's effort and performance. Trust helps us attract higher quality staff[15] and it helps us retain and engage the staff we already have. Without it they disengage, and if they disengage it'll have a dramatic impact on their performance. You'll see a drop in discretionary effort, an increase in accidents and sick days, and possibly sabotage of the work of others.

So, our political systems and economies depend on trust, and organisations' performance relies on engagement which itself is heavily reliant on trust. The bad news, then, is that our willingness

> ### Who can you trust?
>
> In 1960s Britain, 60% of people believed others could be trusted; by 2003, the figure had fallen to 29%.[16]

to trust our leaders and their organisations – even our willingness to trust each other – has been in decline since at least the mid-1990s. This has affected the private and public sectors and even the not-for-profit sector (trust in NGOs dropped from 51% to 30% between 2011 and 2012[17]).

Associate Professor Kevin Money, who is Director at The John Madejski Centre for Reputation, warns us that "Business leaders cannot buy trust, they cannot buy respect, they cannot re-buy their reputations yet they will have to restore them before business can thrive again."[18] More worrying, though, is the fact that those of us who don't trust our leaders find it significantly easier to justify our own dishonest behaviour[19]; the rot is quick to spread.

In summary

The challenge is this: how can leaders tackle increasing demands, complexity and interdependence in a world where people's trust is fragile? The answer isn't a simple one, but – as we'll see in Chapter 2 – the key lies in leadership that is simultaneously Authentic, Responsible and Courageous.

• ● •

2

How ARC can help

• ● •

THE WORDS "Authentic, Responsible and Courageous" will already mean something to you and that meaning will almost certainly evolve as you read this book. To understand how these three qualities can help us deal with the challenges we face, we need a common starting point. So here's what my research suggests these words mean to most people:

- **Authentic:** being true to myself, genuine in my interactions and acting in accordance with my beliefs

- **Responsible:** contributing to the sustained success of the people and things around me

- **Courageous:** overcoming fear in order to do what needs to be done.

How ARC helps build trust

Seven factors[20] determine the extent to which someone else will trust you – whatever your relationship with them.

The first is their general *propensity to trust* – how much they're willing to trust *anyone*. On the face of it, there's not much you or I can do about it. If we're sufficiently Authentic, Responsible and Courageous, though, we can start to work on that system. By role modelling these three qualities and creating a climate and culture that lives up to them, we make it easier for people to trust us and others. You'll also find it easier to **place trust in them**.

The more people we know, the more our networks grow, the more diluted each relationship becomes and the further we drop down each other's lists of priorities. Similarly, as we interact with an increasingly diverse range of people, we often feel we have less **common ground** with those around us. All of these things make it harder to trust. Being Authentic helps us make the most of the time and energy we do have, to forge genuine connections that foster trust. It helps us honestly assess our biases (we all have them) and take control, acting in support of the common good.

Our ability to trust suffers from the pressure on our relationships. These were already under serious strain prior to 2008[21], but with our expectations growing, our population rising and our resources declining, we're increasingly likely to be suspicious of others and selfish ourselves. Being Authentic and Responsible helps us appreciate the pressures others are facing and our contributions to those pressures. This helps us to offer the right kind of help.

Being Authentic, Responsible and Courageous spurs us to challenge those mechanisms that spread the rot of distrust. The skew of news and gossip continues to be towards messages that undermine our trust in others. It's the corrupt officials, corporations, celebrities and sportspeople that tend to get the most coverage. It's leaders' mistakes that attract most attention. Being Authentic, Responsible and Courageous means challenging this hard-wired 'negativity bias' and seeking a *balance* of evidence instead. We should take responsibility for the authenticity of the data we and others use to make decisions and have the intellectual courage to challenge our own and others' biased perceptions.

Being Authentic, Responsible and Courageous also helps us stop the rot by spurring us to challenge others when they're acting in ways that undermine trust. Encouraging others to be Authentic, Responsible and Courageous creates a climate of trust, for the reasons I've given above and because it contributes positively to our predictability, competence, integrity and benevolence.

Your **predictability** or consistency is an interesting component of trust as it triggers something of a paradox. The extent to which we behave consistently from day to day and person to person will affect how much trust others have in us. However, we know from other leadership research that good leadership requires us to treat people as individuals, attending to their own individual talents, needs and aspirations. We'll explore this paradox later when we challenge the assumption that being Authentic means 'being the same all the time'.

When we're Authentic, Responsible and Courageous, we pay due attention to **competence** – critical at a time when people have a lack of faith in leaders' abilities.

The reality is, increasing complexity and interdependence make it harder and harder for leaders to *be* competent. The amount of information available to us is increasing exponentially – in 2006 it was doubling every two years; in 2011 it was doubling every 72 hours[22]. At the same time, we're expected to make increasingly fast decisions. Yes, technology is making it easier to process all that information, but it's not keeping up. Harvard Professor Joseph Badaracco says: "The basic problem-solving principle was 'ready, aim, fire'. Now, we are told, it is 'fire, ready, aim'."[23] Being courageously Responsible involves pushing back against reckless deadlines.

When we're Authentic, Responsible and Courageous, we're honest about our biases, weaknesses and mistakes, rather than ignoring or trying to hide them. We recognise the need to share responsibility and work as a team of people with complementary strengths and conflicting perspectives. We take responsibility for continuous improvement, which demands the courage to stay out of our comfort zones.

Acting responsibly also means ensuring we're mentally and physically capable of making the best decisions. Too many leaders wear ill health and lack of sleep as a badge of honour, but going to work tired has much the same effect as drinking booze for breakfast. Is it any wonder that politicians and wired corporate executives make decisions they come to regret?

Of course, not all of those decisions display a lack of competence: some are lapses in our *integrity*. They're examples of failures to be Authentic, often because we lack the courage to do the right thing. Iraq's information minister Mohammad Saeed al-Sahhaf was laughably inauthentic when he insisted everything was fine despite the sound of battle raging ever closer to the Baghdad radio studio where he was based, and despite the iconic dismantling of Saddam Hussein's enormous statue. Jason Goldberg, co-founder of employment portal Jobster, seemed somewhat inauthentic in 2006 when he dismissed rumours of imminent redundancies while reminding staff to use up their vacation days and blogging that he was listening to songs like "And I'm Telling You I'm Not Going" and Don Henley's "Dirty Laundry" – all just one week before he announced that the company was getting rid of 40% of its staff[24].

We seem to be subjected to a continuous barrage of revelations about leaders' lack of authenticity and integrity.

Failures of integrity

- Only 36% of employees believe top managers act with honesty and integrity[25]

- 76% of employees had observed illegal and/or unethical conduct on the job in past twelve months[26]

- 49% had observed behaviour that, if revealed, would cause their organisations to "significantly lose public trust."[27]

Many news headlines also shake our faith in the **benevolence** of people in positions of power. This is most obvious when it comes to leaders and institutions that are *meant* to be looking after us. Prior to the riots in Los Angeles in 1992 and the death in London of Stephen Lawrence in 1993, for instance, it was generally people on low incomes or from racial minority groups or 'rebellious' subcultures who distrusted their nations' police[28]. Since then, doubts as to police officers' motives are more widespread, and it's far worse in other countries than it is in the US, the UK and the rest of northwest Europe[29].

It's easy to write off benevolence as the domain of public servants and charities, but when resources are scarce it is needed from everyone.

> "The moment there is suspicion about a leader's motives, everything they do is tainted."
>
> Mahatma Ghandi[30]

Just as integrity relies on authenticity, benevolence is founded on responsibility. Now the reality is, the majority of people working in those organisations that have been held up for a lack of competence, integrity or benevolence are decent people who would rather do the right thing than the wrong thing. Only a minority of people are rotten apples, determined to lie, cheat and steal their way to the top. If we're not sufficiently Authentic, Responsible and Courageous, we let those few rotten apples taint the rest of us. Ignoring their behaviour demonstrates a lack of integrity in us. Allowing them to exploit others is an act of malevolence. It's easy to be Authentic or Responsible when there's no downside to being so. It's when manifesting those qualities also requires us to be Courageous that we really demonstrate our right to be leaders.

Some people have chosen to blame business schools for breeding those rotten apples and encouraging those around them to ignore their destructive behaviours. Have we created a generation (or more) of performance-focused, ethics-starved graduates and MBAs? The statistics are fairly alarming (see 'Are business schools to blame?') but business students are far from unique where integrity is concerned. The same researchers found 47% of *non-business* graduates cheated, too[31]. One study found cheating to be alarmingly endemic amongst medical students *and* to be a strong predictor of those graduates subsequently cheating over patient care[32].

Are business schools to blame?

- One sample of MBA students scored no better in ethical dilemma tests than the convicts at eleven minimal security prisons[33]

- Students at twelve top-ranked international business schools in the USA, Europe and Asia were almost twice as likely to choose their future employers based on financial and career opportunities than the company's ethics[34]

- 74% of business students resorted to "unfair" means to get ahead of their fellow students[35]

- 56% of business students (primarily MBAs) actively cheated[36]

Are business schools to blame? Probably no more than other schools. Could they be doing more? Almost certainly.

How ARC helps us thrive in a complex world

Being Authentic, Responsible and Courageous helps us inspire commitment in an increasingly diverse and transient workforce, in spite of ambiguity and continual change. People's willingness to go beyond what is contractually expected of them is highly correlated with the extent to which their leader is Authentic[37]. They're even more committed when that leader is leading out of a sense of responsibility to something bigger than them. Commitment also increases when a leader takes due responsibility for those they lead: ensuring they have the necessary resources, skills and infrastructure to do the job; providing them with opportunities to grow and offering support and protection when required.

Importantly, if they're to commit to something, people need clarity on what it is they're signing up to. Courage enables us to provide that clarity rather than dithering in the hope of certainty in an uncertain and ever-changing world.

As ex-soldier and Sandhurst instructor Anton Horne said when I interviewed him as head of leadership development in one of the UK's largest public sector organisations, "Leadership is about stepping up when the majority of people choose not to." Courageous leaders 'go the extra mile' rather than simply doing what is required of them – and they inspire others to do so, too. It's not enough just to be Authentic: Authentic leaders may build enduring relationships and lead with purpose, meaning, and value, but the research suggests that unless they display courage they may not be described as charismatic or inspirational[38].

Inspiration has three important foundations[39]: 'individualised attention' comes from a blend of authenticity and responsibility, 'intellectual stimulation' draws on a certain brand of courage, and 'a powerful, positive vision' relies on leaders and their people being Authentic, Responsible and Courageous.

It's not just the commitment of our staff that benefits from leaders being Authentic, Responsible and Courageous: we're more likely to gain the commitment of our key stakeholders, too. In a world of competing priorities, connecting authentically with our stakeholders helps us better understand their needs and perspectives. Being Courageous helps us weather the conflicts and challenge each other's preconceptions, and our own.

The three ARC qualities are also a rich source of learning. They help us attend to our competence, as I've said, and they help us attend to others'. Teams and organisations that are Authentic, Responsible and Courageous are more likely to share knowledge in ways that are productive and efficient, and will continually adapt their ways of thinking and working.

Ultimately, though, the aim of commitment and organisational learning is to improve performance. The research suggests that the authenticity of a leader's feedback and interactions with their staff instil high performance behaviours in team members and reduce accidents and formal grievances, all of which drive performance.

Responsibility is also good for business. The benefits of people taking responsibility for their work and the organisation's performance are obvious. However, Harald Harung and his colleagues also found that "organisations based on sound human values and ethics, including CSR, in the long-run outperform organisations where these features are less pronounced."[40]

Courage, too, is a source of competitive advantage. Wherever you're working, your organisation cannot thrive if it is paralysed by the fear of doing something different. It needs to tackle new markets and new customers or service users. It needs to create new offerings and differentiate itself from the herd of similar organisations. Whether it's fuelled by profit, sales, customer surveys, votes, donations, discretionary government spending, or lives saved or improved, it needs to adapt to changes in legislation and the socio-political landscape. Its leaders need to "confront the brutal truth"[41] of its current performance and future prospects and react accordingly.

As one private sector senior manager said to me "In a competitive market, you need to fight." Even in seemingly non-competitive fields like state-funded healthcare and charity work, leaders 'fight' every day for budget and resources. It takes courage to keep on fighting these battles and it takes courage to innovate or take entrepreneurial risks. Nevertheless, as we've seen all too often, courage in the absence of responsibility causes problems.

Courage enables us to challenge each other's perspectives and critique each other's ideas, which drives higher quality outcomes. It's what helps us point a finger at the 'elephant in the room', the 'rotting elk' and 'sacred cows' – those critical organisational issues that all-too-easily go unaddressed. Courage also enables us to hold our people and each other accountable for delivering on our commitments. Yet Courage needs us to be Authentic, too, in our relationships with those people, and for them to be Authentic with us. If we deliver our Courageous challenges while ignoring our responsibility for how they're received, then the people we challenge will simply become defensive.

What you personally have to gain from ARC

If you create a climate that manifests these three ARC qualities, you'll benefit from improvements in your team and in your organisation's performance. There are more direct benefits too, though – purely selfish reasons to be more Authentic, Responsible and Courageous. Firstly, our own performance benefits; research suggests that the more Authentic people are the better they perform in their roles[42]. Goals that include taking responsibility for something bigger than ourselves tend to be more motivating, which increases our chances of success. It might take courage to take them on, but the more ambitious our goals, the more we'll achieve by fulfilling them. Courage helps us deliver on those goals.

Being Authentic and Responsible earns us respect. Being true to ourselves gives us kudos and taking responsibility for something bigger than ourselves gives us the moral high ground. Being Courageous, too, adds something more: when I surveyed nearly 200 middle managers, asking what qualities inspired them when they looked at their own leaders, many cited the leader's willingness to challenge their clients; to them that demonstrated true courage.

If you're focused on career progression, you'll find ARC pays dividends independently of the kudos it brings and its impact on the performance of leaders, their teams and their organisations. In the words of David Dillon, who earns $US12 million a year[43] as ex-CEO and now

Chairman of supermarket chain Kroger: "[Don't] expect the company to hand you a development plan that will take care of everything. You need to take responsibility for developing yourself."[44] That takes courage and a certain kind of responsibility.

It takes effort, too, and ARC can sustain us. Being Authentic saves us energy. Faking it *literally* uses up the body's energy, leaving less to invest in tackling the wealth of challenging decisions and activities that are demanded of anyone in a leadership role. Suppressing our true feelings and beliefs also makes us tense, ill at ease and raises our blood pressure[45]. Combining authenticity and responsibility generally makes us more friendly[46], less defensive and more likely to have close, honest relationships with others[47], which in turn tends to improve our job performance and leave us less susceptible to burnout.

When we're Authentic, people are less likely to seek out our fatal flaws and we're less likely to be worried about anyone finding them. When we're Responsible, we stay on the right side of our administrative, legal and moral commitments and are less likely to destabilise the physical, social and socio-economic ecosystems on which our success and survival depend. When we're Courageous, we're increasingly confident that we can handle whatever life throws at us.

What about all the other admirable leadership qualities?

I'm not rejecting other leadership qualities – far from it. Intelligence, integrity, drive, focus, emotional intelligence and many other qualities are all eminently desirable. So, too, is the ability to establish direction, secure the commitment of staff and stakeholders, and build the capacity of your team or organisation.

In many cases, I believe, being Authentic, Responsible and Coura-geous either produces other popular qualities or relies on them. We saw, for instance, that integrity depends on us being both Authentic and Courageous.

Intelligence is something of an exception. It does contribute to our ability to work with complex systems and hence to aspects of responsibility and courage, but being Authentic, Responsible and Courageous is unlikely to raise your IQ.

On its own, intelligence is a fairly poor predictor of a leader's success, however that success is measured. I believe it's only when used authentically, responsibly and courageously that intelligence really makes a positive difference. When governments and individuals accumulate dangerous levels of debt, it isn't generally stupidity that's to blame; it's a lack of responsibility. Why do so many leaders fail to do what their intelligence or moral compass tells them to do? Because their courage fails them.

In summary

While each quality is powerful in its own right, the true strength of Authentic, Responsible, Courageous leadership lies in the way the three qualities interact to be 'more than the sum of their parts'. They help build trust and equip us to deal with a world of increasing demands, complexity and interdependence. They also help us demonstrate other desirable leadership qualities. As we'll see once we've explored each of the qualities in depth, the three ARC qualities together offer a simple but formidable tool for making difficult leadership decisions.

● ● ●

How best to use this book

• ● •

THIS BOOK EXISTS for five key reasons:

1. To show how desperately the world needs its leaders to be Authentic, Responsible and Courageous

2. To make it clear what's in it for you – because very few of us are utterly selfless and I think it's important that we accept that

3. To explore the reasons why it's hard to be these things – the challenges in each and the tensions between the three – because I'm here to work *with* you, not judge you

4. To help you overcome those challenges and tensions

5. To leave you with something simple but rich – as David Cannon from the London Business School said when I first introduced him to the ideas in this book, we can instantly assess the extent to which we're being Authentic, Responsible and Courageous in a given situation, *and* we can explore each of those three words in enormous depth should we choose to do so.

The book is structured to achieve these five things. We'll cover each of the three qualities in turn. We'll look at what it means to be Authentic, Responsible and Courageous, what makes it hard to be these things 100% of the time, and I'll offer suggestions aimed at helping us be more ARC. As we go, we'll increasingly bring the three together to help you negotiate the tensions between them. Then we'll look at how we master that 'dance' and we'll work out what you do next in order to apply what you've read to the world in which you work.

You'd never become an Olympic swimmer simply by reading about it, though, and the same is true of leadership. You'll get much more from this book if you actively engage with it by taking due time to answer the questions it poses, to examine how ARC applies in your workplace, and to challenge your preconceptions. Use whatever it takes to embed your learning. Write in this book or in a notebook, discuss it with others and, if you'd like to, download additional resources by visiting the "How we think" page at www.leader-space.com.

You'll be encouraged throughout to set goals for yourself. My hope is that you'll do so, but don't overstretch. One of the most common mistakes in leadership development is that people underestimate how difficult it will be to change. It's really easy to make a commitment to being Courageous when you're sitting on a train or a plane reading a book, or sat at home with a glass of wine in your hand. It's much harder when the moral dilemma rears its head and the pressures of work, your career and your family commitments are upon you. I'd like you to be ambitious and committed to getting something useful and lasting from this book, but if you ask too much of yourself you'll quickly lose interest.

● ● ●

"Even if
you win the
rat race, you're
still a rat."

William Sloane Coffin[48]

PART
2

Authentic

4

What do we mean by 'Authentic'?

• ● •

AT THE AGE OF SEVENTEEN I was working in a newsagent in a leafy, sleepy, well-to-do suburb of London.

One hot sunny September day, while a small, slight and unassuming lady called Anne stood behind the counter serving the slow trickle of customers, I busied myself on the shop floor refilling some shelves.

Suddenly, I heard a loud shout behind me. I spun around to see a young man at the counter, facing away from it. He had cash in his hand – notes he'd clearly snatched from the till. "Who wants some?" he was shouting. "Who wants some?"

I rushed towards him and grabbed him in a bear hug. He broke away and I kicked out as he fled. Then I noticed a strange, warm feeling on my left arm and looked down to see a slow, thick trickle of blood oozing down my arm. At first, I thought he'd scratched me, but within seconds the trickle became a torrent. By the time the ambulance arrived I was barely conscious. By the time the surgeons had closed the wound, I'd spent six hours in intensive care, they'd pumped 24 pints of blood through my system and I'd apparently 'died' twice.

And I never even saw the knife.

Years later, I have three scars from a total of 70 stitches and I can still feel pain in parts of my arm. I can't feel or properly use some fingers due to the nerve damage sustained. While I've never had panic attacks or suffered from post-traumatic stress, I *am* overly sensitised to potential threats in public places. It's a heightened sense of vigilance rather than fear. It doesn't make me anxious but it has stimulated a different kind of curiosity. No surprise that I subsequently trained as a criminal psychologist!

I wouldn't change what happened. That single event reassures me that I'm the kind of person who stands up for what they believe is right. I 'died' for what I believed in – that stealing is wrong – and lived to tell the tale.

The most common misconception was that I was brave. I've since realised that it wasn't bravery at all: brave people see the danger and do it anyway. They overcome their fears and press on. *I never even saw the knife.*

So what was I doing? What was I *being*?

I was being Authentic.

I'm no paragon of virtue and I don't 100% embody this one quality all of the time. I certainly don't manage to consistently manifest all three of the qualities I'm writing about.

Of course I don't. But being Authentic is, in part, about understanding our flaws. It's also about giving of ourselves, bringing our whole selves to the work we do and the lives we lead rather than pretending we're automatons or gods, able to influence the world without it influencing us.

Authenticity defined

A lot has been written about authenticity in the past few years – particularly with regard to Authentic leadership. I find myself disagreeing with quite a lot of it. For instance, I believe:

1. The meaning given to authenticity in leadership literature does the word a disservice. I'm not alone – Susan Scott in her book *Fierce Leadership* expresses concern "that this word [authenticity] is used so frequently that it has lost meaning and impact, and that's a shame, because authenticity is a big deal when it comes to hiring people with the capacity to connect with their colleagues and customers."[49]

2. Most leaders are too busy to spend time wading through leadership theory and research. We need to keep things simple – to maintain purity in the meaning of authenticity while at the same time reflecting the complex reality in which these people operate.

It's in their attempts to reflect that complex reality that I believe the promoters of Authentic Leadership have set traps for themselves. We all know that simply being Authentic isn't sufficient for great leadership. We all know that authenticity comes at a price. We all know that sometimes a price is paid by the leader, sometimes it's paid by the led, and sometimes it's paid by both. I believe this is a challenge we have to accept.

One writer who falls into the trap is Bernard Bass. If you've read or been taught anything on leadership, he probably had an influence on it – you may, for instance, have heard of transformational leadership which was big in the 1990s and still endures, with good reason. To me, there's something inherently wrong in the following statement from a piece by Bass and his colleague Paul Steidlmeier: "authentic transformational leaders may have to be manipulative at times for what they judge to be the common good"[50]. The idea of authenticity incorporating manipulative behaviour simply doesn't work for me.

A similar example comes from Rob Goffee and Gareth Jones. They have a lot of great things to say, about authenticity and about leadership. However, they refer to the "highly-honed art" of sharing weaknesses selectively. I believe that what they are talking about there is something *other* than being Authentic. To my mind, it's an interaction between authenticity and responsibility. If a leader reveals things about himself that undermine his people's faith in his ability to lead, he may be failing to live up to one of his responsibilities as a leader, as followers need faith in their leaders. Although, of course, if he really *isn't* fit to lead, telling people this (and finding a replacement) might well be the Authentic *and*

Responsible thing to do. This is a prime example of the 'dance' between authenticity and responsibility.

I've settled on four ways in which we are either Authentic or not – Four Spheres of Authenticity.

Authentic *Action* and Authentic *Interaction* cover the things people generally suggest first when I ask them to define authenticity. Authentic Action encompasses statements like "You don't become a better leader by becoming more like someone else"[51] and "a visible connection between what you believe, what you say and what you do".[52] It's there in our willingness to behave in alignment with our personal values[53] rather than reacting to external threats, inducements, social expectations or rewards[54].

Authentic Interaction is what happens when leaders are genuine, present and transparent. It's there when people do not have to speculate about what the leader is 'really like'[55]. As one article puts it "Leadership begins when you stop blaming others or making excuses"[56], "when we realise that making mistakes or falling short of our intent only makes us human"[57]. Authentic Interaction also involves the leader being "Clear about what he [or she] stands for and believes in"[58].

The research suggests Authentic Actions and Interactions depend on two other Spheres of Authenticity. Our actions are more likely to be Authentic if they're grounded in Authentic *Intent* – a sense of purpose rooted in our core values. Naturally, we're not always as Authentic as we intend to be. It's because of this that we need Authentic *Insight* – the ability to own our "personal experiences, be they thoughts, emotions, needs, preferences, or beliefs"[59].

These Four Spheres of Authenticity can be tricky to grasp at first, so I've come up with the following definitions...

AUTHENTIC ACTION

Acting in accordance with our Authentic Intent, rather than reacting to external threats, inducements, social expectations or rewards. Demonstrating a visible connection between what we believe, what we say and what we do.

AUTHENTIC INTERACTION

Being genuine, present and transparent in our relationships with others, rather than presenting a façade. Communicating in ways that make it clear what we stand for. Being honest about our opinions, flaws, mistakes and contributions (good and bad).

AUTHENTIC INTENT

Approaching life and leadership with a sense of purpose that is drawn from our core values and beliefs. In the short term, this means honestly appraising our intentions for a given situation. In the long term, it involves us aspiring to be the best version of ourselves that we can possibly be.

AUTHENTIC INSIGHT

An honest, non-judgemental appraisal of our own strengths and weaknesses. Recognising and understanding our habits, motivations, emotions and perspectives, including understanding their origins and their effects on our behaviour. Appreciating the fact that some of our deeply held attitudes, beliefs and assumptions contradict each other. Taking ownership for the way we respond to situations.

The following case study shows the Four Spheres in action. It also offers some insight into how all three ARC qualities interact when we're making leadership decisions.

A couple of years ago, 'Eduardo', the head of the Dutch office of a mid-sized multinational decided to consolidate the company's office space which was spread across four locations between Amsterdam and The Hague. He called in his four direct reports to announce his decision. The four offices were to be merged into one, central to all four locations. His four direct reports, whom I'll call Amber, Bob, Charles and Dhanjit, reacted in four different ways:

1. Amber said nothing to Eduardo or her three peers. She returned to her team and told them what 'the boss' had decided. They reacted with the usual range of emotions – anger, fear, despair. She reacted by sharing her own misgivings, the guilt she felt as the bringer of bad news and the person in charge of making the move a reality.

2. Bob reviewed the conversation on his way back to his own office, then called Eduardo for further clarification on the rationale and proposed implementation of the move. Afterward, he called a staff meeting and delivered the news, the rationale and the plan with all of the conviction Eduardo would have had. He convinced them all, but didn't believe a word of it.

3. Charles went through a similar process to Bob, only his wife encouraged him to spend time identifying what it was he *did* agree with in the rationale and proposal. In doing so, he realised that the decision to move offices made sense from a business angle. He realised, too, that he and the team were getting too comfortable in their current location, that they were starting to stagnate in their careers and that the move could be a catalyst for change.

4. Dhanjit was the only one of Eduardo's four reports who stayed behind after the meeting that Monday morning. She challenged Eduardo over the decision, sharing her own concerns and the likely reactions of her staff. It was a robust, challenging discussion for both of them but they agreed some compromises and sweeteners that Dhanjit could take back to her team.

Which of these four team leaders is being Authentic?

Leaving aside any debate over which approach is *right*, I believe the only one who *isn't* being Authentic is Bob. Amber's Interaction with her staff is Authentic to a point, because she's being honest with them and revealing her own vulnerability. Charles's starting point is different. Rather than jumping straight in at the top, focusing on Authentic Interaction, he starts with Authentic Intent. Instead of simply taking a one-sided view of the situation, he looks for ways in which Eduardo's proposal *does* work for him. He finds the good in it, rather than assuming it's all bad. He doesn't *invent* benefits, like Bob does, but Charles does look for ways in which the proposal is aligned with what he genuinely believes in. This takes him down into Authentic Insight, where he recognises and challenges his own desire to stay within his comfort zone. His subsequent interactions with his team are then at least as Authentic as Amber's. They're also more productive and take account of the responsibilities he has as a team leader, which aren't simply to the team he's leading. Amber's sense of responsibility is far narrower and thus her authenticity is far more self-centred.

And what about Dhanjit? Dhanjit has drawn on her courage, and challenged the proposal. This has helped her be Authentic in her Interaction with Eduardo. She is also taking greater responsibility for her team than Amber did.

Authenticity and consistency

In leadership, being consistent is important. It can certainly be difficult for staff, shareholders and other stakeholders when a leader suddenly changes their approach or direction. Many of us have worked for leaders who habitually switch to a new strategy before we can implement the last one.

At the same time, being Authentic is *not* necessarily about being consistent over time. In its purest form, being Authentic is about being true to oneself. Like it or not, that 'self' is not a single, consistent thing: it is constantly evolving. We cannot help but be affected by the world around us. We are created by it, and constantly recreated.

We're not physically consistent: not one of the cells in your body today was there ten years ago. And we're not mentally consistent: research shows that we don't have a single and reliable thread of memory uniting us with the person we were before. Our brains habitually create incorrect memories within seconds. They spot any holes in what we've seen or heard, and then fill the gaps to create a seamless narrative.

One author, echoing Buddha and the philosopher David Hume, described our 'self' as "an ever changing collection of beliefs, perceptions, and attitudes that is not an essential or persistent entity but a conceptual chimera."[60] Personally, I think that's an extreme and potentially disheartening view of ourselves. I find it more helpful to take Daniel Goleman's perspective:

> "Past self-images leave their trace: no one has just one fully integrated self-image, a single harmonious version of the self. Various points and stages in life accrue overlapping selves, some congruent, others not... A gangly, isolated adolescent can become a svelte, gregarious thirty year old, but the svelte self does not completely eradicate traces of the gangly one."[61]

In order to be truly Authentic, we have to embrace this personal evolution. Our bodies, minds, attitudes, beliefs, memories and knowledge change over time. To be true to myself I need to appreciate this, but I also need to know myself well enough to understand the difference between a momentary blip and a lasting change of perspective.

A blip could be a short-term reaction to some external event. Maybe I'm upset because my favourite team lost an important game, or I missed the train to work, or a client shouted at one of their staff in front of me. Maybe I'm suffering from a 24-hour illness or one-too-many drinks in the bar last night. A lasting change of perspective might come from an article that shifts my view on the way we do business, or something I learned on a course last week. Perhaps my mother or my child has fallen ill, causing me to re-evaluate the way I structure my life. Bill Gates, of Microsoft, is a classic example of this kind of authenticity in action. In the early 1990s, Gates is quoted as believing the Internet was too resource-hungry for the computers of the day. He predicted that its popularity would grow at a slow rate and that the Internet wouldn't be of practical use until 2010. So Microsoft invested modestly.

Then came Netscape, the world's first commercially successful Internet browser. Netscape cornered 90% of the market earning it a market value of US$2.9 billion by the end of the first day's trading. Had Gates remained consistent, he would have stood by his prediction. Instead, he focused on success, on the future. He left his ego behind him, adapted his position and Microsoft came out fighting. Whatever your opinion on Gates, his company or his products, there's no denying the scale of Microsoft's victory over Netscape.

Being Authentic is difficult. Very few people are determined to be *inAuthentic*, but then very few people are determined to increase their carbon footprint. We'll look at why it's so hard in the next chapter. Before we do, though, I'd encourage you to consider your own authenticity...

QUESTION 1 Complete the following sentence with as many distinct points as you can.

"There are times when my actions and interactions are entirely Authentic. For instance, I…"

QUESTION 2

For each of the examples you listed in Question 1, what was it that enabled you to be Authentic? *(It might help to consider who you were with, what you were thinking and feeling prior to acting authentically, and what you assumed about yourself and others going into that situation.)*

....

....

....

....

....

....

QUESTION 3

Given that being Authentic relies heavily on our personal values, what are yours? *(I recommend using the exercise in Appendix 1 if you're not 100% clear on your values. It'll challenge you, but it's worth it.)*

....

....

....

....

....

....

In summary

Authenticity starts with us being honest with ourselves – with Authentic Insight. From this springs Authentic Intent, which is rooted in our values. For the most part, it's only when our intentions produce Authentic Actions and Authentic Interactions that our authenticity makes a difference to the world around us.

● ● ●

5

Why it's hard to be Authentic

• ● •

ONCE UPON A TIME, I gave what I thought was a robust presentation as part of an interview process for a job that had never existed before. I'd been asked to apply months before and during that time the job had changed and for me none of the changes were positive. At the end of the presentation, my potential new boss said "I'm not sure how much you really want this job."

My guts murmured quietly in response to a sudden clash of conflicting and contradictory emotions. Unfortunately, I rose to the challenge. My brain told my mouth how to solve the problem it *thought* it was meant to be solving.

I got the job.

I say 'unfortunately' because, a few months later, I quit. I didn't leave for a better job with greater responsibility and a better salary; I went back to the job I'd had before. I'd known all along that this wasn't the job for me and I'd loved the job I'd left. If I'd been Authentic when my new boss gave me a chance to opt out in that interview, I'd have saved myself, and others, a lot of wasted effort.

Everyone has been less than completely Authentic at least once. We've all failed at times to be straight with a client, colleague, boss or family member.

50% of Europe's full-time workers say they behave significantly differently at home from the way they behave at work[62]. Of course they do: most people make some attempt to project a positive image of themselves in the workplace[63]. They do it because it earns them more power, greater autonomy, higher salaries and bonuses, and better outcomes in performance appraisals[64].

Some of the data suggests this has gone too far, though: that such a stark differentiation between our 'work selves' and 'home selves' is unhealthy. The figures vary greatly by culture, even within Europe (e.g. 64% in the UK say they behave significantly differently, versus 36% in the Netherlands). Adapting our behaviours is one thing; feeling we have to *be* a fundamentally different person is another. That route leads to a workplace where everyone is a fraud.

Our failures to be Authentic are totally understandable. We're all complex creatures. There are three main reasons we're inAuthentic: habits, roles and fear. If we understand them, we've a greater chance of overcoming them.

Habits

Sometimes we're inAuthentic by accident. It's not intentional: we just get carried away by other forces and it's only in retrospect that we find ourselves out of sync with our values, beliefs or the person we feel we could (or should) be. Other times, we do it on purpose. We tell a white lie. We spin the truth or we pay someone else to do it on our behalf. We tell people what we think they want to hear, or what we feel they need to hear in order to give us what we want.

We learned to do this when we were children. It's how we got the grown-ups to give us stuff – whether it was toys, time, love, autonomy or forgiveness. By the age of seven, we'd built our core repertoire of techniques – our most successful survival mechanisms. We practised them through our teens and took them, as hard-wired habits, into adulthood. And now we're leading teams, departments, businesses, charities and governments using those same survival mechanisms. No wonder it can feel like primary school in the boardroom.

What's important, if we're to be Authentic, is to recognise that those childhood behaviours wouldn't have become habits if they hadn't proven valuable. It's only by understanding the value they bring that we can ditch the behaviours that make us inAuthentic.

Our habits don't just interfere with the authenticity of our Actions and Interactions, though; they can get in the way of Authentic Insight and Intent. Many of us move so swiftly from one event or conversation to another that we don't have the time to review what just happened or prepare for what's coming next. We fixate on our Blackberries or iPhones as we walk from meeting to meeting, conversation to conversation. We get caught up in the details and our need to please others. We're so busy working fast and hard that we can't afford the time it takes to understand what we're doing, and how and why we're doing it. And these habits have generally worked for us; just like running 'works' for the hamster on his wheel.

Roles

We each play numerous different roles in life, wearing a number of different hats. Each role brings with it certain responsibilities, introducing tension between authenticity and responsibility. Perhaps 'parent' is one your roles in life. Perhaps that role has made it hard for you to pursue the aspirations you had in your 20s. Perhaps you've responded by refining those aspirations and feel you've left part of your Authentic self behind in the process.

Or maybe you've been in the role of 'middle manager', where the competing expectations of those above, below and around you encourage you to act like a different person in each interaction.

The role of 'leader' is a particularly challenging one – intellectually, physically and emotionally – and places great strain on our authenticity. As leaders, we will almost certainly become figureheads, idolised or demonised as the focus for other people's hopes and fears, for their aspirations, insecurities, expectations and personal failings. This blurs our Authentic Insight: it becomes harder to distinguish the 'real' me from the role we're inhabiting, with all of the baggage it brings. The further up the hierarchy we go, the higher the stakes and the more our seniority acts like a force of gravity, attracting all the complexities and conflicts in the world around us. We become Responsible for things we can't control, don't fully understand and maybe don't even notice.

These challenges show us sides of ourselves and others we might not have expected. They can make it hard to form an Authentic Intent and to translate that Intent into Action. In addition, as we become more senior, people's perceptions of us become more polarised. We become increasingly two dimensional and stereotypical in their eyes, and more complex in our own. This disparity makes it harder to have Authentic Interactions.

Fear

Habits and roles are important, but I believe the primary barrier to being Authentic is fear. If we're to overcome those fears, we need to understand them. With this in mind, I'd like to offer up some common fears based on my own experience of coaching hundreds of leaders and on the wealth of research into our needs as human beings[65]. They're not meant to be exhaustive but just enough to get you thinking, and perhaps discussing them with others.

The first four fears are fairly straightforward, so I'll offer just a few examples…

- I'm afraid of being judged as **stupid**, so I avoid sharing my true opinion and risking someone proving it wrong; or admitting I don't know the answer; or I take steps to disguise the flaws in my project or proposal rather than being honest about them

- My fear of people thinking I'm **selfish** means I avoid sharing my priorities or doing what is important to me

- My fear of being considered **cruel** means I avoid pointing out flaws or giving feedback in front of others

- My fear of seeming **weak** means I avoid sharing my mistakes or concerns, or revealing that I'm not indomitable.

There's a real tension between the remaining two fears on the list – the fear of being **different** and the fear of being **the same**. We all need to feel different *enough* to reassure ourselves that we're unique, but not *too* different from others that we feel isolated and alone.

Organisations tend to homogenise, or standardise, their people – either because their leaders recruit clones of themselves or because the strength of an organisation's (or team's) culture squeezes out diversity.

We risk being ostracised if we seem to fit a stereotype that the majority don't like. I see this a lot in organisations that favour a more stereotypically 'masculine' management style characterised by assertiveness, task-focus, harsh critique and aloofness. In these organisations, women who inauthentically adopt a more masculine style suffer; they have to pretend to be someone they're not and, if they do it well, they're branded with another stereotype: the 'ball busting alpha female'. Unfortunately, women who naturally (i.e. authentically) favour a more "masculine" leadership style are often accused of being insufficiently feminine – sometimes even inauthentic.

Each of these six main fears is centred on the fear of being judged and found wanting and, as a result, being rejected or persecuted, exiled or preyed upon. This is just as true when we believe we're *choosing* to fake it. If someone lies to you or pretends to be someone they're not in order to influence, ultimately it's because they're afraid that they'd fail to get their way if they took a more Authentic approach.

Fear can be incredibly powerful and it's understandable that many reveal their true selves with caution.

How fear reduces Authentic Insight and Intent

Plenty of people are afraid of introspection. It can seem weak to question ourselves, self-indulgent to spend the time it takes to do it. We might be afraid of what we'll find there: that we'll be forced to confront some of the cruel or stupid things we've done, that we'll lose ourselves in the confusion of contradictory beliefs and emotions, that we'll be isolatingly different from the people around us or that we're not as special or unique as we want to be. Some of us are afraid we won't be perfect, or that we'll disappoint someone, everyone, or maybe just ourselves.

In creating an Authentic Intent, we might be afraid our aspirations are unrealistic, idealistic, clichéd or unprofessional. Or we might be afraid we'll lack the skills, intelligence, selflessness, willpower, connections or charisma to turn that Intent into Action.

All of these fears are understandable, but let me make one thing clear: by encouraging you to develop greater Authentic Insight and Intent I am not calling for you to vanish into your own inner world never to reappear. In my experience, Authentic Insight is best focused on the present. Any exploration of the past is best done to understand the way we're thinking, feeling and acting *now*. Critically, we need to accept that it is our *current* relationship with past events that defines us. Too many people become overly focused on blaming their upbringing; this isn't helpful, it's usually destructive and takes a long time to fix. It robs us of control over who we can be.

QUESTION 4

In order to understand what makes it harder for you to be 100% Authentic, complete the following two sentences. Try to be as specific as possible and complete each sentence with as many distinct points as you can.

a. **"There are times when I'm not truly Authentic. For example, I..."**[66]

....

....

....

....

....

....

....

b. **"I do the things in Question 4a because if I were to do the opposite, I'm worried that..."**

....

....

....

....

....

....

....

In summary

Being Authentic isn't always easy. Our habits and the roles we play can get in the way. So, too, can fear: fear of being rejected or persecuted because others think we're weak, cruel, selfish or stupid. Perhaps they'll see how different we are, or how similar to an unpopular stereotype. Sometimes even the prospect of being honest with ourselves stirs up those very same fears.

• ● •

6

Six routes to Authentic leadership

● ● ●

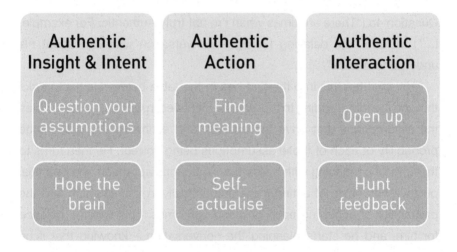

Authentic Insight & Intent	Authentic Action	Authentic Interaction
Question your assumptions	Find meaning	Open up
Hone the brain	Self-actualise	Hunt feedback

THE SIX SUGGESTIONS

above are options. Trying to action all six at once can be overwhelming, so I'd recommend choosing two or three to start, then come back for more when you're ready. Bear in mind that the actions that most repel you will probably be the ones that will make the biggest difference if you do them properly. It's like investing when the stock markets are performing badly: there's so much more to be gained than when shares are at their peak.

OPTION 1: Question your assumptions

The fears you listed in response to Question 4, at the end of Chapter 5, were underpinned by certain assumptions about yourself and your environment. If we're to tackle those fears we need to tackle the underlying assumptions. I often use a process that draws on a fantastic book called *Immunity to Change*[67]. We'll work through an example, shown in the table over the page, then you can have a go yourself in the blank table that follows.

In our example, Mark is a middle manager whose responses to Question 4a ("There are times when I'm not truly Authentic. For example, I...") include "am delaying having a conversation with Jim about his underperformance".

He's written this into the first box in the table below. He then works through the table, adding to the fears he identified in Question 4b. He notes the assumptions that drive those fears, and estimates the percentage probability of each of those assumptions being correct. He then turns to the risks of continuing with a less-than-Authentic approach, the potential positive outcomes of acting more authentically in this situation and the probability of achieving each of those outcomes. This tips the balance for him, and he starts planning the conversation – knowing that if he connects authentically with Jim, he'll increase his chances of achieving those positive outcomes.

1. **I'm being less than Authentic by:** Delaying having a conversation with Jim about his underperformance

2. **I'm doing this because I'm afraid the following would happen if I was more Authentic:**
   - I'll upset Jim
   - He'll be less motivated
   - He'll quit
   - The rest of the team won't like me

3. **In thinking these things could happen, I'm assuming:**	4. **Probability of these assumptions being correct:**
I'll deliver the news in a way that'll upset him	50%
He's motivated at the moment	20%
The feedback won't motivate him to change	50%
It's a bad thing if he quits	40%
The team will like me more if I allow Jim to continue underperforming	25%

5. **By acting less than entirely Authentic here, I'm risking:**
   - Losing my team's respect and trust
   - Underperforming as a team, which will affect our morale and draw unwelcome attention from my boss

6. **If I were to respond to this situation more authentically, it might produce the following positive outcomes:**	7. **Likelihood of achieving this outcome:**
Jim will accept his performance is sub-standard and work to improve it	40%
Our performance will improve, which will improve morale in the team	60%
The team will respect me more	60%
My boss will see that I can deal with underperformance	40%

YOUR TURN

1. **I'm being less than Authentic by:**

2. **I'm doing this because I'm afraid the following would happen if I was more Authentic:**

3. In thinking these things could happen, I'm assuming:	4. Probability of these assumptions being correct:

5. **By acting less than entirely Authentic here, I'm risking:**

6. If I were to respond to this situation more authentically, it might produce the following positive outcomes:	7. Likelihood of achieving this outcome:

OPTION 2: Hone the brain

"Brain power is to the information age what iron, coke and oil were to the industrial age – the one necessary ingredient on which all else depends."

R. E. Kelley[68]

In 2009, a particularly important paper[69] was written on the link between our brains and the way we lead. It was written by two experts in neurology and an associate professor in the engineering faculty at Oslo University College in Norway. This seminal research paper didn't just state the obvious (that a certain amount of intelligence is required to lead effectively), it found links between the physical features of a person's brain and the quality of their leadership.

Like others before them, Harald Harung and his colleagues refer to the pre-frontal cortex as the "CEO" of the brain. It's the part of the conscious brain that ultimately makes the decisions. The pre-frontal cortex is thought to balance our morals, personality, needs and long-term goals in order to respond to whatever's happening in the present. When we're extremely stressed, this internal "boss" of the brain is effectively switched off and the less sophisticated parts of our brain take over – kind of like the inmates taking over the asylum.

Our brains are continually developing, through a series of physical changes that capture and store our various experiences. Brain scans[70] showed that one key difference between "world-class leaders" and Harung and Co's average performing control group was that the former showed greater "brain integration": their brains stored new experiences in a way that was more integrated with existing knowledge and experiences. Basically, the CEO in the brain was much more effectively and efficiently connected with the brain's various other departments. The brains of these leaders used much less time and energy when accessing relevant information to make decisions. The researchers also found more 'alpha wave' activity in the brains of exceptional leaders when they were given various tasks.

Alpha waves (electrical currents with a frequency of around 7.5-13 cycles per second) are believed to occur when we're integrating disparate data into a coherent whole – a critical component of good leadership. These brain waves are also associated with a mental state that combines high alertness with inner calmness. Interestingly and importantly, given our current focus on authenticity, Harung and Co's research also suggests that "brain integration may be the physiological basis of personal integrity".

So how do we help our brains integrate new information more efficiently? One way is to increase the number of 'peak experiences' we have. These are akin to the 'flow states' frequently reported by exceptional athletes, musicians and artists – periods of time when we experience an inner calm, playfulness and curiosity while being incredibly focused. We feel fully integrated in ourselves and everything feels right – we're not caught up in second-guessing ourselves or worrying about the past or future. Exceptional, Authentic leaders experience more of these states than the average manager. These peak experiences are generally accessible in one of two ways – through becoming more 'self-actualised' (which we'll cover shortly) or through meditation.

Regular meditation or related 'mindfulness' practices greatly increase the proportion of alpha waves. Over 600 published research papers[71] report a range of benefits – reduced stress levels, greater resilience, enhanced academic achievement and productivity at work, major health improvements, improved creativity[72] – to the extent that America's National Institutes of Health provided over US$24 million to fund further research[73] and the UK's National Health Service embraced mindfulness training as part of its treatment regimen. There's also been a lot of recent research into the use of mindfulness in schools[74], suggesting that regular practice can undo the level of attention deficit many 21st-century parents see in their kids.

It only works if you do it regularly. Practitioners' recommendations vary, but tend to fall in the range of 3-5 times a week, for 15-40 minutes a time. I'd probably recommend you find a regular slot in your working day when you can create 15 minutes of undisturbed time – perhaps your daily commute is a good time. Don't bother with the weekends – that could come later when you start to enjoy the benefits and want to do more.

As little as an hour a week for 12-14 weeks can reduce stress, help us sleep better, improve heart performance and help stabilise the autonomic nervous system[75] – the part of our nervous system that controls our bodies' recovery from physically and psychologically demanding activities.

You can even download apps that offer tailored mindfulness programmes and exercises as short as 3 minutes – Buddhify and Headspace are good examples. I can't formally endorse either until I've seen empirical evidence of their effectiveness, but psychologists are looking into it and apps like these work for me. Bear in mind that it takes an average of 66 consecutive days to form a habit[76], so you'll probably find this challenging at first. But, with any form of meditation, you should see some initial benefits within a couple of weeks – and once you're past the first 2-3 months it'll be part of your routine.

OPTION 3: Find meaning

> "He who has a why to live for can bear almost any how."
>
> Friedrich Nietzsche

Viktor Frankl was an Austrian-born neurologist and psychiatrist. He was 34 at the outbreak of the Second World War and living in his native Vienna. As a Jew under Nazi rule, he was only allowed to treat Jews and was given the dubious distinction of Head of Neurology at the only hospital left open to Jewish patients. He worked there, specialising in brain surgery, until 1942 when he, his new wife, his brother and his parents were sent to a concentration camp. He spent time in four camps between then and his release at the end of the War in 1945, including Auschwitz. His father died of starvation in the first camp; his mother and brother were killed at Auschwitz; his wife died at Bergen-Belsen in the last few months of the War. Of Frankl's immediate family, only his sister Stella survived – she'd emigrated to Australia shortly before.

As a psychiatrist, Frankl closely observed the differences between those who survived the holocaust psychologically as well as physically. The survivors, he found, were the people who were able to find some kind of meaning in their new environment – however horrible it was. They didn't cling to the old ways and they found a new way of living that was true to them.

Sometimes, as middle managers or team leaders, we don't fully buy into the new way of doing things. In such situations, we can opt for one of four courses of action:

- Question the change

- Reject it and side with other resistors

- Fake it – as Bob did when he pretended to buy into his boss's directives

- Find what it is in the new way of doing things, or the journey to get there, that is meaningful and Authentic.

The fourth of these options is consistent with Frankl's observations. A far less dramatic example is my own experience of being asked to take on an unexciting project at a time when I didn't have the luxury of refusing to take it on.

> **"Follow your compass and not your clock."**
>
> Ann Moore, CEO of Time Inc. and Board Member at Avon[77]

I could have spent my time complaining about it to my wife, my friends and colleagues and anyone else who'd listen.

I could have faked it and pretended I was interested in what I was doing. But neither of these was a healthy, honest or sustainable way forward.

Instead, I looked for the meaning in what I was doing, and really surprised myself. There were genuine reasons the project worked for me and they included:

- the client aspired to do something that was 'best in class' and it was certainly the best example I'd seen

- the kudos I gained from working with that client

- the quality and diversity of the participants I worked with

- the project's reliance on feedback and coaching, which are activities close to my heart.

Connecting with these gave me a natural, genuine energy for the project that I know from feedback came through in the way I interacted with everyone. If I hadn't found some personal meaning in the project, then frankly I'd have been rubbish. I'd have lacked the energy to deal with the lack of sleep, gruelling days and long-haul flights. I'd have lost the sense of humour that helped my team and me through all manner of challenges, and the people I was leading would have seen right through me.

Finding meaning also increases our authenticity. People need to see that we believe in the things we're selling them. They need to hear the authenticity of our Intent in the tone of our voice, see it in our eyes

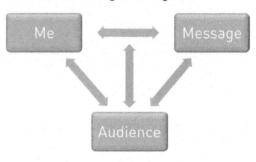

and the subtle changes in our facial expression – changes only the most accomplished actors can fake. Consider the Authenticity Triangle[78] above. My role as a leader is to get my Audience (the people I lead) connected with the Message (the thing I'm trying to get them to do or buy into). As I'm going to be around for a while (I hope), I need to create a connection between them and Me, their leader. For them to really commit, my Audience needs to see that I am personally connected to the Message. If I've found real meaning for myself in the Message they'll see it, without any acting on my part – although it'll be easier if we Open Up as suggested in Option 5 (below).

OPTION 4: Self-actualise

The concept of self-actualisation[79] has been around since the 1940s[80]. It appears at the peak of Maslow's famous pyramid depicting the hierarchy of our needs as human beings. Self-actualisation can help us realise our potential as human beings.

Self-actualisation is typically defined as a combination of[81]:

- Living a balanced life, where the various parts complement each other (rather than one dominating)

- Setting ourselves stretching personal goals and striving to achieve them.

Unfortunately, it seems very, very few people manage to achieve self-actualisation – less than 1-2% in research conducted by a Harvard academic[83]. One reason for this is that people tend to focus either on personal goals or on their aspirations to make the world a better place. Rarely do they focus on both.

Many people fail to realise that both sides of self-actualisation are highly relevant to leadership; ignoring or hiding one in favour of the other is inAuthentic and detrimental. Being self-actualised, or at least working proactively towards it, makes us more rounded, raises our self-awareness and boosts our self-esteem.

A quick rant about self-actualisation (optional reading!)

Maslow's model has been criticised due to a lack of empirical evidence that the needs existed in a hierarchy. More recently, the original model – familiar to many psychology graduates, MBA students and participants in leadership programmes – was redesigned to reflect advances in evolutionary biology, anthropology and psychology[82].

The new hierarchy, published 40 years after Maslow's death, drops self-actualisation in favour of finding and keeping a mate, and using them to procreate. Parenting is the new peak experience. Hmmmm…

Now, don't get me wrong: I love being a parent, but do I believe passing on our genes is the summit we should all be striving for? Maybe at the level of hard, mindless and soulless biology, but when it comes to being the best version of ourselves we can be, or bringing our own unique contribution to the world? In my opinion, while it may be pretty old as a concept, self-actualisation is still very much on the table.

Self-actualisation is a particularly difficult thing to learn from a book but, in the interests of giving you something here that you can use, start with the following… Review the last typical week you had and complete the table over the page[84].

When you're done, try the following exercise (suggested to me by Professor Peter Hawkins[85]): fill an A4 or letter-sized sheet of paper with things you want to be remembered for (Question 5). Keep going until you've filled the space. Then circle or highlight the five that are most important for you. Do not take the obvious shortcut of simply generating five things you want to be remembered for as it's often only once we build up momentum that we discover what's really important to us (and you *will* gain momentum). Once you have your five, move onto Question 6 and work out a way that those five could be a self-sustaining virtuous circle – i.e. how can these five priorities support each other to help you be all you can be?

Area	Current satisfaction with this area (0-10)	Hours spent enjoying/improving this area per week*
Creative/artistic expression		
Family		
Fun		
Intimacy		
Growth/personal development		
Personal finances		
Physical environment		
Physical health and fitness		
Professional development		
Sleep		
Socialising/time with friends		
Spiritual well-being**		

* Maximum total in one week = 168 hrs. Don't go crazy trying to get a precisely accurate figure, but don't just guess, as you'll probably be wrong

** This means whatever you take it to mean. It needn't relate to any specific or formal religion

**Two ways I could realistically increase
my satisfaction in this area**

QUESTION 5

I want to be remembered for... *(fill an A4 or letter-sized sheet of paper, then write down your most important five here. The blank space may seem daunting but you'll build up momentum.)*

....

....

....

....

....

....

QUESTION 6

The virtuous circle. Once you have your five priorities from Question 5, work out how those five can be a self-sustaining virtuous circle. Ask yourself "How can these five priorities support each other to help me be all I can be?"

....

....

....

....

....

....

OPTION 5: Open up

Once upon a time, during a period of economic recession, I was interviewing one of the owners of a UK company with thousands of staff in front of a handful of his middle managers. Knowing that the middle managers were feeling isolated and over-stretched, I asked a question about the extent to which – once you're at the top – you still feel the need for support.

Like many highly paid executives before him, he shared how lonely it was at the top of an organisation. As he talked, though, I remember thinking how he was probably far less isolated than some of the executives I've met in my travels. Why? Because he was so candid and good humoured in the way he spoke. *This*, I reckoned, *is a man whose Authentic Interactions will help ensure he's never truly alone at the top.*

It occurred to me afterwards that he needn't be at the top at all. The expression 'at the top' brings to mind images of standing alone at the summit of some mountain. It's a very hierarchical, status-oriented stereotype of leadership. More helpful, particularly where authenticity is concerned, is to realise that the more authority we're given the closer we get to *the centre* of everything that's going on in our organisation. And in the centre, we're never alone, although sometimes we might prefer to be!

Participants on most good leadership programmes have some very Authentic Interactions with each other. They open up *a lot.* Initially, the fear of being different holds them back. But once they start sharing what's really important to them – their values, their origins and their challenges – they discover how much they have in common.

When we come to the end of a leadership programme, so many groups say how lucky they are that that particular group of people came together – that this precise constellation of individuals was formed for that particular period of time. But it's not luck. Sure, very occasionally someone prefers to send their 'professional self' on the programme and leaves other aspects at home, but rarely. What participants sometimes fail to see is that they can create similar experiences with anyone they meet. It's what happened in the *relationships between* these people that made this great experience happen, not *who was in those relationships*.

Importantly, though, 'opening up' isn't just about sharing our ambitions and aspirations, our feelings, hopes, fears, mistakes and so on. It's about more honest communication – communication that draws on Authentic Insights into ourselves. We spend a lot of our time speaking in code, rather than saying exactly what we mean.

German psychologist Friedemann Schulz von Thun[86] says in order to decode the *real* messages in people's communications with us, we need to identify and distinguish between:

- the **facts** they're sharing with us

- the **appeal** they're making to us

- what's being said about our **relationship** with that person

- what that person's words (and the way they deliver them) **reveal** about them.

One simple way to understand this is with reference to a statement you probably heard from your parents: "Your room is a mess." If you hear the statement from a 'factual information' perspective, you treat it as data. You assess whether it's true, relevant and complete as a package of information. Thus a suitable response would be to say "Thank you, I hadn't noticed" and continue playing. If you hear it from the 'appeal' perspective, you read the command embedded within the statement: "I want you to tidy your room." This presents you with a choice: do you do what they're asking you to do, or continue playing? To make this decision, you might take the 'relationship' perspective, which gives you access to your parent's attitudes towards you. This often comes through in the precise choice of words or the tone of voice: "Your room is a mess *again*" implies certain things about your attitude to tidiness that "Your room is a little untidy" does not.

The 'relationship' perspective also encrypts data about the other person's assessment of your relationship with them, which can be encoded in the way they speak, the words they use and/or the history you share.

Finally, the 'revealing' layer tells you things about them. There will be data here that they're intending to send you and data they probably aren't. Their tone tells you they are frustrated – perhaps because they believe you're ignoring them, or because they're afraid some imminent visitors will interpret your messy bedroom as a sign of inadequate parenting.

Why am I introducing this model here? Because encoding all this data in the hope that others will decode it reduces our capacity for Authentic Interaction. It increases the risks of miscommunication and misunderstanding, which in turn reduce the chances of us gaining true commitment from the people we're leading. More effective and Authentic is to notice the data we're encoding and choose to decode it ourselves before we transmit it to others.

OPTION 6: Hunt feedback

The average person thinks they're better than around 75% of their peers. At work, at least, this effect increases as the actual level of performance decreases[87]: the less able a person is, the more likely they are to overestimate their abilities. It also increases with the person's seniority in the organisation[88] – the discrepancies between leaders' self-ratings and other people's ratings of them getting bigger and bigger and bigger. There may be a few reasons for this, but the most straightforward contributor to this lack of self-awareness is the fact that, as we get more and more senior, we get less and less access to feedback[89].

Knowing oneself is a prerequisite to being Authentic. There are really only two ways to achieve this: introspection and feedback from others. Few leaders do enough of either. Typically, we're focused on getting the job done, juggling all manner of priorities to achieve what we're paid to achieve. This is totally understandable. But when we're focused 100% on keeping those balls in the air we're missing opportunities to learn. It's like the apocryphal story of the logger who is too busy to stop and sharpen his axe.

How often do you, your staff and your colleagues stop to sharpen your axes? Are you using feedback as effectively as you might? Too many of the organisations I've worked with rely solely on their performance appraisal system as a source of feedback. It comes maybe once or twice a year and the feedback is written not verbal.

Did you ever learn to drive a car? Imagine your instructor saying "I can give you feedback as we go – I'll tell you when you need a little more clutch or a lighter touch on the brake – or every few weeks I'll write down everything I can remember and send it to you in an email."

A lot of people say they're open to feedback. Some really mean 'praise'. I've given a lot of feedback over the years and I know most people are receptive. The key issues are:

1. *Few people actively seek feedback*. They wait for it to come to them rather than hunting it out.

2. When they do ask for feedback, *people are often unclear what they want* from the exchange – it can be much more helpful to the person giving feedback if the recipient tells them what kind of things they want feedback on.

3. *People often react to the feedback in ways that discourage the giver* from continuing to give. For instance, rather than absorbing feedback or asking for more information, many people react by justifying their behaviour.

4. *People don't always ask the right people*. The majority of men, for instance, want their feedback to come from above[90], however, sometimes there are other people better placed to provide constructive feedback.

So, if you're interested in knowing yourself better, I'd encourage you to hunt out that all-important feedback. Be proactive; be persistent; be focused in specifying the kind of feedback you want. At the same time cast your net wide to ensure you're looking for feedback in the most appropriate places and be graceful and inquisitive when you receive it.

In summary

If you're keen to be more Authentic, there are lots of routes on offer. I've suggested six and encouraged you to try three to start with. Questioning our assumptions reduces the fear that gets in the way of being Authentic. Mindfulness helps us know and manage ourselves more effectively in the moment. Finding meaning and self-actualisation connect us more with what matters to ourselves. Opening up and seeking feedback creates more Authentic connections with others and raises our awareness of ourselves.

• ● •

7

Questions and commitments

• ● •

I'M A BELIEVER IN questions being the true route to a deeper understanding of oneself. So, consider and discuss the following:

You

- In each of the spheres of my life, to what extent do others experience me as Authentic?

- What climate/culture do I want around me?

You and your team (or family)

You can either answer these questions yourself, or use them as discussion points for a team meeting.

- To what extent are we as a team (or family) being our true selves at both an individual and unit level?

- To what extent are we clear what we (as individuals and as a group) believe in?

- Choose three people who are close to you at home or work. Looking at each one individually, what forces make it hard for them to be Authentic? Then ask yourself:

  - What am I doing to contribute to this?

- What forces in their relationships with others or the type of work they do make it hard for them to be Authentic?

- What baggage have they brought with them (their beliefs, assumptions, identity, upbringing, fears, etc.) that makes it hard for them to be Authentic?

Your organisation

- What are we doing as an organisation that our staff can see is Authentic?

- How Authentic do we seem to our external stakeholders? If we don't already know, how might we find out? What answers might we expect? What would we do with the information?

Your commitments

- Make one big commitment to yourself (in relation to being Authentic) and write it down.

....

....

- Clarify your commitment:

a. Who else is it important to?

....

....

b. Why is it important, to you and to them?

....

....

- Identify 3 significant people in your life (at work or otherwise) and make this commitment explicitly to them. *(Obviously, you could wait until you've finished the book before you do this, but I strongly suggest you share your commitment before reading on. Who should you choose? People that matter to you, whose opinion you value, who would notice quickly if you strayed from your commitment, and who will be both fair and brutally honest.)*

● ● ●

PART

3

Responsible

8

What do we mean by 'Responsible'?

• ● •

BEING RESPONSIBLE is about looking beyond ourselves. We all have different responsibilities. Sometimes they conflict with each other, and sometimes they get in the way of our efforts to be Authentic. Some of our responsibilities are matters of ethics – a banker's responsibility to the world economy, a doctor's responsibility to his or her patients, an energy company's responsibility to the natural environment and vulnerable customers in colder climates. Others are personal – our responsibilities to our loved ones and our communities.

Managing our own responsibilities is challenging, yet more complex is what happens when ours rub up against the responsibilities of others. Where should we step aside and let others take over? Where should we jump in and help?

There has been much research into 'diffusion of responsibility' or 'bystander apathy' – an effect, common in many organisations, where individuals fail to take responsibility because of the presence of others who could potentially take it for them.

In northern Iraq in 1994, two American F-15 fighter planes accidently shot down two American Black Hawk helicopters, killing all 26 military and civilian personnel on board. This incident was so controversial that it was investigated not only by the US Air Force itself but also by the US Senate *and* the House of Representatives. According to Professor Scott

Snook, at the United States Military Academy, responsibility was "spread so thin... that no one felt compelled to act"[91].

You'll see it at a trivial level in any office, too. It's there when everyone complains that the coffee machine isn't working but no one tells someone who can actually do something about it. It's there when the Board of Directors recognises there is a fundamental issue with the culture of the organisation but none of them takes action to change it.

Three Stages of Responsibility

Taking responsibility is a three-stage process. We need to:

- **Realise** there's something to be Responsible for

- **Prioritise** – to decide where that responsibility sits relative to other responsibilities

- **Act** according to our prioritisation.

For example, let's say a major stakeholder calls you right now and tells you she needs a specific report by Friday at 4pm. Ten minutes ago, you didn't *Realise* there was anything to take responsibility for – your client needed the report, but you weren't aware of that need. You have a lot of other things to do by Friday afternoon and your diary is full. You need to choose whether your responsibility to deliver this report is higher *priority* than the other responsibilities on your plate. If you decide it *is* higher priority you need to *Act* by rescheduling, delegating or cancelling the things that will get in the way.

Being truly Responsible as leaders requires us to overcome potential obstacles at all three of these stages.

First, though, I'd like to share something that helps me and my clients Realise the full extent of our responsibilities.

Realising:
the Three Domains of Responsibility

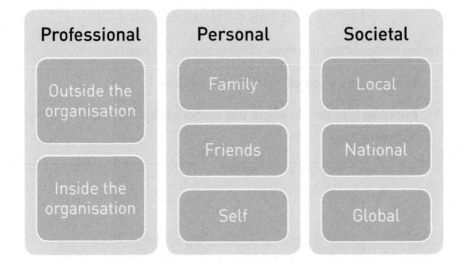

Professional	Personal	Societal
Outside the organisation	Family	Local
	Friends	National
Inside the organisation	Self	Global

Professional responsibilities

"Any of us can figure out ways to drive a business for two years and make a boatload of money and move on. That's not leadership. That's playing a game. Leadership is leaving something lasting, whether it is how you treat people or how you deal with a problem."

Ann Fudge, Chair and CEO of Young & Rubicam[92]

Responsibilities outside your organisation

Your responsibilities to people, institutions and things outside of your organisation will vary depending on your role and the nature of the

Outside the organisation

- Our target market: customers, clients, end users, etc
- Investors/shareholders/owners
- Analysts/media
- Unions
- Suppliers and partners
- Our labour market
- Our legal and regulatory obligations
- My profession
- My future employers

Inside the organisation

- The thing I'm here to do
- The shared endeavour
- The organisation
- Its history
- Its culture
- Its people
- Its processes
- My staff
- My boss

organisation itself. They will probably include at least some of the items in the list above. You'll have your own perspective on each of these but, if they exist in your operating environment, you will be Responsible to and for them – in some capacity. Neglecting those responsibilities is what causes many organisations to fail.

Responsibilities inside your organisation

Some of the responsibilities above will benefit you; some will feel like a burden; others you may not even realise are having an impact on the way you lead.

"**The thing I'm here to do**" is the primary purpose of the job for which we're employed – maybe it's obvious, maybe it's not; maybe it's never been explicitly stated; maybe it's a moving target; maybe we have to dig deep to work out what it is.

Responsibility to **"the shared endeavour"** is a critical extension of "the thing I'm here to do" when we're working in teams. Individual team members are generally focused on their own results – the feedback they'll personally get from their boss, a customer or client, the score they'll get in their performance appraisal, their commission or the bonus they'll get at the end of the year. Responsibility shifts the focus to *shared* results – what the team achieves, or the organisation, or what's achieved through a partnership with some other person, department, division or external body.

This sense of a shared purpose changes our decision-making when the pressure is on, when time and money are tight and we're competing for resources. It also allows leaders to delegate not just to individuals, but to relationships, without the destructive 'diffusion of responsibility'. For example, a CEO could delegate responsibility for increasing profitability to *the relationship* between the Finance Director, Sales Director and Director of Operations. If she makes it clear that they will *all* fail and be held to account if the organisation doesn't hit its targets, she's much more likely to get a good result than if she makes each of them Responsible for a separate piece of the puzzle. Experience tells us that those separate pieces quickly become pieces of turf – three corners with a director in each, fiercely defending their territory against intrusions from the others.

By being Responsible to **"the organisation"**, I mean specifically as an entity in itself – distinct from its component parts (its people, its assets and so on). As leaders, we have a responsibility to ensure that our organisations are healthy and sustainable, that they're well managed and have good reputations with external stakeholders. A shame, then, that so many leaders lose sight of the long term when there's trouble in their target markets – and it seems that the bigger the organisation the more short-term its leaders' perspectives become[93].

When I ask the leaders I work with what they believe their responsibility is to **their organisation's people** and **their own staff** (or 'followers'), their responses fit into one of three categories:

- Health and safety

- Learning and development

- Morale and motivation – including giving due recognition and taking 'flak' to protect the team.

When it comes to investing in *learning and development*, the leaders I've spoken to are keen to keep growing their staff – although they admitted they weren't always as good at doing so as they might be. They talked about helping their staff stay in their 'stretch zone' – far enough out of their comfort zones to be learning, but not so far that they panic.

Morale and motivation have been a real challenge over the past few years. In the UK, for example[94], between September 2008 and September 2011, the percentage of UK workers stating that their jobs were insecure or very insecure doubled to almost 50% (and reached 63% for women). Short-term optimism entering 2012 was still significantly lower than in Sept 2008 – a distinctly uncomfortable climate for anyone of working age, whether they've got a job or not.

At the same time, the leaders of these organisations became increasingly task-focused at the expense of relationships with their people. In the language we're using to describe responsibility, they prioritised the task over the people. Research conducted by consultancy colleagues of mine[95] late in 2011 showed that 45% of staff said their leaders had become more task-focused. Only 9% said their leaders had become increasingly people-focused.

You might think ups and downs in morale are cyclical, that morale waxes and wanes with the local or global economy. However, this doesn't seem to be the case. The UK workforce had been growing increasingly dissatisfied since the mid-1980s[96] and was the second most dissatisfied workforce in Europe back in 1995[97]. And in the USA there has been a steady decline in job satisfaction since the 1970s[98]. Is it the proliferation of computers and other technologies that's had this terrible effect on our lives? No. Statistically, where you live, your connectedness with your customers, your level of autonomy and the quality of your relationship with your boss are the most important factors in determining how satisfied you are at work[99]. And, the evidence has shown – time and time again – that happier workers *are* both healthier and more productive[100].

The responsibility of leaders for **the culture of their organisation** (or individual departments or teams) is something we've heard a lot about in recent years. When the atrocities at Iraq's Abu Ghraib and Camp Bread Basket came to light, for instance, we asked whether the military (and political) leaders who ordered monthly checks on the facilities were doing enough to fulfil their responsibilities. When scandals erupted over expenses claimed by British MPs, it arose that misuse of public funds was a cultural rather than individual issue.

The Professional responsibility people often find hardest to accept is the responsibility they have to **their superiors**. CEOs and politicians are frequently being told that they should resign because of the failures of their staff. Rarely are staff asked to resign because of a failure on the part of their leader – unless it's by the leader themselves, who has nominated them as a fall guy or scapegoat!

Being Responsible to our superiors

When I talk about being Responsible to superiors, I'm not just talking about getting work done on time and achieving the objectives our bosses set for us. I'm talking about looking out for them, helping them succeed and anticipating the challenges they're likely to face – both practical and emotional. In the words of a report on trust by the UK's Chartered Institute of Personnel and Development...

> "The nature of followership also has to change: what's needed is an attitudinal shift on the part of employees from being dependent upon leaders to also seeing themselves as responsible for

creating a positive workplace climate. Benevolence
should become a two-way relationship with
employees becoming more benevolent towards
new leaders and not blaming new leaders for
the mistakes of their predecessors. "[101]

Boards and their shareholders still hire and fire with alarming frequency in their search for the perfect CEO. Teams still hang their hopes on their next boss and then find themselves disappointed. Ultimately, no matter how great an incoming leader is, he or she will come up against the 'immune system' of their new team or organisation – the team or organisation's prevailing beliefs, attitudes, behaviours and so on. The new leader is like a skin graft, or an organ donated for the good of the host body: only if the immune system accepts the newcomer will he or she succeed in doing the job they need to do.

Responsibility certainly falls on the leader to convince that immune system that he or she is not some dangerous virus. However, I believe far too little responsibility is taken by our teams and organisations for over-riding their immune systems to help ensure an incoming leader's success. Far too little attention has also been paid to the role of followership in organisations (Barbara Kellerman's book[102] being one notable exception). We spend billions on leadership training, but I know of only one type of organisation that teaches people how to follow: the military. To most people, the very concept of followership training is anathema. Think about it: would you ask to go on a course to learn how to follow? Would your HR department dare to run one? Try asking the question. At best you'll get a confused response; at worst, an angry one.

I'm not proposing turning people into mindless automatons, but I *am* interested in the fact that we're so resistant to the very idea of training people to follow. We can't all be leaders, after all. There will always be far more followers; most leaders are themselves followers. And yet we're expecting people to know instinctively how to follow.

Realising our Personal responsibilities

Australian singer, song-writer and compulsive blogger Bronnie Ware has written a book called *Top Five Regrets of the Dying*[103] based on her years spent as a nurse providing palliative care to patients in the last 12 weeks of their lives[104]. What's either reassuring or terrifying is that the Top 5 regrets are desperately predictable.

I'll cover the others later, but Number 2 on the list is "I wish I hadn't worked so hard." Apparently, "This came from every male patient that I nursed. They missed their children's youth and their partner's companionship. Women also spoke of this regret, but as most were from an older generation, many of the female patients had not been breadwinners. All of the men I nursed deeply regretted spending so much of their lives on the treadmill of a work existence."

In 2001, 85% of American workers said they'd like more time at home with their family[105]; 46% wanted 'much more time'. In the UK the latter figure was a little lower at 36%. We could guess how these figures might have changed in the interim, but they're a good starting point, and there is data for 23 other countries.

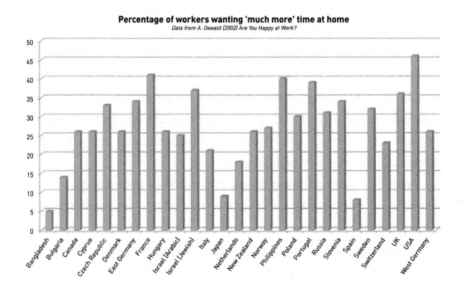

Percentage of workers wanting 'much more' time at home
Data from A. Oswald (2002) Are You Happy at Work?

The fourth most common regret in Bronnie Ware's list is "I wish I had stayed in touch with my friends." She speaks of her patients' sadness in their final weeks when they realised they hadn't made the most of the friendships they'd had. They'd been distracted by life's other pressures – that long list of competing responsibilities – and hadn't invested sufficient effort in the people who really mattered to them.

While most of us take responsibility towards others seriously, clearly we should invest in being responsible to ourselves, too.

1. ***Looking after ourselves in the present:*** to manage our energy levels and ensure we have sufficient capacity to achieve what we're committed to. This is something even President Bill Clinton managed to do: he says he'd take an hour in the middle of each day for himself and would spend two hours a day reading for pleasure. He says the worst decisions he made were generally during times when he'd failed to maintain that regime[106].

2. ***Looking after our 'future self'*** – the 'me' of 10, 20, 30 years' time. This isn't just about self-actualisation but simple sustainability, or survival. Are you working so hard that you're taking 10 years off your life? Have you spent the first 20 years of your child's life putting cash in the bank at the expense of getting to know them?

One final note on personal responsibilities: Ronald Heifetz, Alexander Grashow and Marty Linsky, authors of *The Practice of Adaptive Leadership,* note that we're often affected by our sense of responsibility to "people from the past with whom you identify who have shaped how you see the world, such as a revered grandparent or a special teacher, as well as the groups of people who form your gender, religious, ethnic, or national roots."[107] Even when these people have ceased to exist as anything but memories, our sense of responsibility to them remains. It motivates us and affects our decision-making, but can also be a source of conflict with other areas of responsibility. I recognise, for example, that the death of my father when I was seven left me with an insatiable drive and a potentially dangerous subconscious attitude that one parent is enough for any child – an attitude that could make me less Responsible at home.

Realising our Societal responsibilities

The past 10-15 years have seen a seismic shift in people's perceptions of interconnectedness and, with it, a shift in their expectations of leaders' and organisations' Corporate Social Responsibility (CSR). A generation or two ago, CSR was on few leaders' radars; only a few philanthropists realised they had any responsibility whatsoever. In the 1990s, we thought it was 'nice' if our employer donated money to charity or provided us with recycling bins. Now, CSR is included in many companies' procurement processes and annual reports. For some, it's still little more than a marketing ploy but, with Generation Y considering CSR a hygiene factor, that cynicism is fading. Between 2008 and 2011, in percentage terms, companies typically cut their spending on salaries and research and development harder than they cut their investment in CSR[108]. They've not only *realised* their responsibilities, they've *prioritised* them.

As Peter Senge and his co-authors say in *Presence*[109], our increasing interconnectedness means many of the negative social and environmental side effects of our actions manifest on the other side of the world. A corporate decision made on one continent can change lives on another. We fail to see the effects our lives have on other people, then fail to understand them when they rise against us. Diffusion of responsibility is literally costing the Earth, and you and I are to blame.

In the 1960s, we were using about 60% of the world's resources to sustain us as a species. Only a few countries – including the UK, India, Ethiopia, Cambodia, Spain, Portugal, Norway and Germany – were using more than their land could provide. In 2010, globally, we were using around 150% of the Earth's sustainable capacity. The USA, China, Europe, Russia and most of North Africa had all slipped into the red. By 2050, given population projections and the way our expectations are increasing, we'll need at least two Earths to sustain us – and that's using the most conservative United Nations' estimates, assuming population growth slows and our diets improve a little. The vast majority of countries living within the earth's means are African; quite a few are Asian; one is European. Only seven countries come close to achieving what the UN deems 'high levels of human development' without exceeding their fair share of the world's resources.[110]

If our planet was a business, the shareholders would be looking to invest elsewhere. Our staff would be looking for new jobs, knowing redundancies and liquidation were a hair's breadth away. Our suppliers would be getting their bills in quick and stressing over repeated late payments. Our customers would be laughing at our three-year warranties and promises of technical support, knowing we'd not be around long enough to fulfil them. And our CEO and his Board would be facing a judicial enquiry. The CEO, of course, would blame the previous CEO and the incompetence of the directors he inherited. They'd all say they did what they could but there wasn't enough cash in the market and their staff were more focused on status, camaraderie and keeping their hours down – rather than delivering the kind of results their inflated salaries demanded. In six months' time, the company would either have gone the way of Lehman Brothers or a new CEO would have grasped the nettle, made some major changes and turned things around.

We know there's a problem, so why aren't we all doing more to deal with it? Sure, it's complicated, but why is it that, as diffused as it is, there's not currently enough responsibility in the system to save the system from itself?

This may sound like a call-to-arms or a guilt-trip, but – like being Authentic and Courageous – being Responsible is about making personal choices. I'm not trying to get you to quit your job and join an NGO in Angola. I'm not saying you should spend your evenings patrolling the streets picking up litter. I'm not even saying you need to spend more time with your family and friends. I'm saying we all need to make conscious choices when it comes to responsibility.

Global interdependence means all of us have an effect on the world at three Societal Levels (local, national and global) and across three Areas of Responsibility (economic, social and physical/environmental). In some cases, we'll be having a negative impact. There's certainly an argument that says we don't need to be Responsible *for* all of these areas, but we are Responsible *to* them, and – if we're to lead in the way that's required in the coming decades – we do need to avoid being *irResponsible*. All too often, our actions (or lack of actions) are the result of long-established habits, or a lack of awareness, or a failure to prioritise what we truly believe is important.

Interactions between the three domains

As you'll probably have noticed, some of our choices in the personal and professional domains can have an effect at a societal level. Take, for example, the social and economic effect of longer working hours on local communities.

I was born in London, but I now live in a much smaller city. The area I live in is as middle-class and middle-income as the places I've lived in London, but people's working patterns are very different. A lot work in creative or helping professions. A lot more are self-employed. Very few work days as long as the majority of people I know in London, and the community benefits enormously. Our street has a vibrancy I hadn't experienced since I was a kid. People know each other, regardless of their age or their choice of career. They chat in the street, invite each other into their houses, hold big parties for their neighbours as well as their (other) friends and they congregate *en masse* on Friday nights at one of the local pubs.

It also helps that the vast majority of parents pick their children up from school at 3.30, rather than from after-school care at 6pm or later. This makes 'play dates' more likely, bringing children's parents together as well as the children themselves. Additionally, picking kids up directly from school means parents arrive at the same time – rather than whenever their commute allows them to – which offers still more opportunity to interact.

These are some of the social benefits of a change in working practices.

The economic side effects include people doing a lot of their shopping locally, because they have time and want to contribute to their community – because they feel more connected to it. People also pass on unwanted items for free, rather than selling them on eBay.

And so it goes on. It isn't utopia, of course. But it got me thinking about the impact our working practices have – not just on the people we employ, not just on their families if they have them, but on the communities in which they live.

In summary

Being Responsible is primarily about looking beyond ourselves and takes place in three stages. We need to:

- **Realise what we're Responsible for**

- **Prioritise our various responsibilities**

- **Act accordingly.**

The more interdependent we become, the broader our network of responsibilities. Realising the full extent of our responsibilities requires us to consider three Domains of Responsibility:

- **Personal – including our friends, family and ourselves**

- **Professional – stakeholders within and beyond our organisation, including some people, institutions and more abstract concepts like an organisation's history and culture**

- **Societal – the economic, social and physical needs in the local, national and global systems that sustain us.**

● ● ●

9

Why it's hard to be Responsible

• ● •

"Hope for human survival and progress rests on two assumptions: (1) human constructive tendencies can counter human destructive tendencies and (2) human beings can act on the basis of long term considerations, rather than merely short term needs and desires."
Howard Gardner, Harvard University Professor of Cognition and Education[111]

WHEN WE FAIL to be duly Responsible, it's because we have stalled at one of the three Stages of Responsibility: we didn't Realise, we didn't Prioritise, or we didn't Act. There are reasons for each.

Failing to Realise

One man who failed to realise the full extent of his responsibilities was Japanese General Tomoyuki Yamashita. In 1945, he was tried for atrocities his troops committed in internment camps in the Philippines. His defence was that he hadn't visited the camps in question. Nevertheless, Yamashita was hung – not for those things he did, and not for the things he knew about, but for the things he *should* have known about. This 'Yamashita principle' still holds today and it has been the death knell for the careers of numerous leaders.

There are four key reasons why you might fail to realise you're Responsible for something:

1. **It's not in your 'line of sight':** things come on to your radar when you're too busy to deal with them

2. **You miss the details:** it's easy to miss crucial points when you're working under pressure

3. **You fail to 'read between the lines':** you don't pick up hints and don't see problems heading your way

4. **You fail to see the wider context:** the majority of us (particularly in Western cultures) are more focused on the details and discrete components than on the 'bigger picture'; maybe you've been oblivious to an entire stakeholder group whose needs and commitment are critical to your success.

Failing to Prioritise

The Three Domains of Responsibility we covered in Chapter 8 should help you realise and redefine your responsibilities. Often, though, it's our *prioritisation* of those responsibilities that causes us to be less Responsible than we could be. Maybe at work, to get results or maximise our profits, we bend the rules or overstretch our people. Or to get ahead (or for the sake of our sanity), we put our own agenda ahead of our team's or the organisation's. Or we fail to deliver on a deadline or promise, or fail to chase others hard enough to ensure they follow up on their commitments.

Maybe we 'pass the buck', shifting the blame for mistakes or misdemeanours to someone else – or we delegate work or tough messages *up* the chain of command. Maybe we promote a culture of 'presenteeism' that damages the quality of everyone's work.

Perhaps we're only half-present in the time we have with our family. We keep checking our Blackberries, iPhones or whatever. Maybe it's the same when we see our friends – *if* we see our friends – and maybe we ignore the impact our purchasing habits have on the environmental and socio-economic fabric in which we live. Not always, of course, but when we're in a hurry or wrapped up in other things.

The way we prioritise the competing demands on our time and energy is personal to each of us. At the same time, though, it's not always logical, or even conscious. Like much of our decision-making, it's driven largely by emotions and immediate needs, rather than a long-term perspective.

I've come across five main reasons for avoiding responsibility, each of which has nuances of its own.

I can't do it

a. **because I don't have sufficient time, resources or 'bandwidth'**

b. **because I lack the skills, intellect or ability.** We're afraid we'll fail, do it badly, or make the wrong decisions – perhaps to the detriment of our reputation, the cause or the people involved.

I shouldn't do it

a. **because it's none of my business.** You worry about being seen as 'interfering' or a 'control freak' if you seek additional responsibility

b. **because of what it might cost me.** Standing by while someone dies would leave a psychological mark on most of us, but we might choose to do so if coming to their aid means we risk sustaining a fatal injury ourselves.

Someone else will do it

a. **because ultimately it's their responsibility.** Maybe it's the people above us, whom we feel should be better role models for responsibility themselves. Or maybe  it's the direct reports we're trying to empower by delegating to them

b. **because there's no reason I should make the first move.** This is the essence of 'bystander apathy' or 'diffusion of responsibility'. It's closely related to the phenomenon of 'social loafing': generally, as the size of a group increases, the effort put in by each individual member of the group decreases.

I don't want to do it

a. **because I don't have the interest, motivation or inclination.** This is exacerbated by the decline in the "psychological contract" between employees and their employers in recent decades – the psychological contract being the unwritten contract  between an employee and their employer; the informal, unspoken beliefs that each has about their responsibilities to each other[112]. Since the 1980s, perhaps earlier, we've seen a loosening of the ties of responsibility people feel towards their organisations and co-workers

b. **because the potential recipient doesn't deserve it.** You don't feel moved by the plights of others, or have become inured by endless news stories of tragedy and feel removed from the issues. Perhaps here diffusion of responsibility is rearing its head again: someone else will sort it.

c.   ***because it's just not me.*** Taking on responsibility for some things can seem out of character to us – at odds with the way we see ourselves.

I can't decide right now

Sometimes we lack the necessary information to help us prioritise one thing against another. For instance, should I support the struggling farmers of other nations by buying from them, or reduce my carbon footprint by buying local produce? This creates a kind of "cognitive gridlock", at which point we could:

1.   gather more data

2.   make a decision based on limited information

3.   postpone the decision and move on.

Sometimes, Option 1 doesn't seem viable. Option 2 gets us moving but could leave us with the wrong order of priorities, which produces one of two outcomes:

a.   we lack full commitment to our espoused responsibility (and fail to follow through as well as we might) because we're always aware that we didn't do our homework properly

b.   we cling dogmatically to our decision, filtering any new data to support our choice and resisting any attempts to change our mind.

Option 3 (postponing the decision and moving on) either prevents action on the responsibilities in question, or leaves us oscillating between one responsibility and another – our actions contradict each other. For instance, one day I buy local to keep my carbon footprint down, the next I buy from a cash-strapped South American cooperative so I'm contributing to the lives of people 'less fortunate' than myself.

Market societies and the 'systemiser skew'

Two interlinked phenomena are interfering with the way we Realise and Prioritise our responsibilities: 'market societies' and the 'systemiser skew'. In addressing the former, Harvard Professor Michael Sandel[113] argues that capitalist market economies have been great for growth and brought us a whole host of benefits (albeit often at someone else's expense), but that by failing to put boundaries on capitalism, we've created cultures where you can buy pretty much anything.

In some countries, you can buy a place at the front of a queue, whether it's for a rock concert, an airport or a seat in a government hearing. You can literally pay an organisation that pays a homeless person to hold you a place for 24 hours then hand it over at the last minute so you can waltz in and take your seat. You can advertise almost anywhere – in prisons, on people's bodies, in children's books and games. You can buy the life insurance policy of a stranger so that you pay the premiums and you cash in when they die – hopefully soon, as that'll increase your return on investment. And parents have grown used to paying their children to do well at school and to do jobs around the house that in the past would have been a moral obligation – or just an act of kindness to help Mum and Dad. Turning our kids into little capitalists from as young as four years old is a real blow to responsibility. The research strongly suggests that one of the best ways to destroy a person's intrinsic motivation to do something is to pay them to do it. We're at risk of skewing our children's decision-making patterns and attitudes to responsibility.

This skew is easy to see through the lens of one of the world's most commonly used models of personality, the Myers-Briggs Type Indicator (MBTI®[114]). Based largely on the work of Carl Jung, one of history's most famous psychiatrists, the MBTI draws a fairly blunt distinction between two styles of decision making, stating that we all use both but that each of us favours one over the other. More recent research suggests each style is driven by different systems in the brain, which cannot operate simultaneously[115].

One style ('Thinking') focuses on logic, objectivity and the practical utility of the various options; it sees fairness as a matter of treating everyone equally. The other style ('Feeling') prioritises values, relationships and personal perspectives; fairness is about understanding each party's individual needs. Psychologist Simon Baron-Cohen[116] makes a very similar distinction but uses the terms 'systemisers' and 'empathisers'.

Baron-Cohen's take is intentionally provocative, greatly favouring the empathisers. In reality, there is a great deal to be said for both approaches and for striving to achieve balance and healthy tension between the two styles.

The problem is, this balance doesn't exist in the workplace.

It's partly because of long-term gender imbalance in positions of power. The MBTI data and Baron-Cohen's studies suggest that 60-70% of men are systemisers and 60-70% of women are empathisers. Baron-Cohen concludes that: "Since most political systems were set up by men, it may be no coincidence that we have ended up with political chambers built on the principle of systemizing."[117] Most organisations around the world share these same 'political systems'. Sure, women are gradually becoming more common in senior roles, but it's a painfully slow process and their career progression is (or appears to be) largely dependent on favouring (or pretending to favour) a systemising decision-making style.

It's far harder for women, or men, to get promoted for being empathisers. There's a certain irony in this: when I asked over 170 middle managers which of the leaders above them they found inspiring and why, 51% of the behaviours they cited were characteristic of an empathising style – trusting, being supportive, focusing on relationships, and so on.

It seems that by failing to manage the boundaries between our economic principles and our social/cultural principles, we're tipping the natural balance and creating a system in which people are less likely to take on certain kinds of responsibility.

Failing to Act:
"I realised and prioritised, but didn't act"

I've seen this countless times: people commit to decisions, insist they're extremely important and they fail to follow through on them. Why? Lack of self-control or self-discipline, perhaps? An underestimation of how difficult their chosen course of action might be? Distraction? Fear? Self-doubt?

It could be any one of those, yet all too often we're falling into a pattern of behaviour. If our reasons for failing to act are typically ones we've used before, whose origins lie in our personalities more than the world around us, there are only two *real* reasons for getting stuck between 'prioritising' and 'acting'. Either our prioritisation wasn't sufficiently Authentic, or we lack the courage to act.

In summary

When we don't respond Responsibly, it's because we

- failed to realise the extent of our responsibilities – maybe we overlooked a detail, failed to read between the lines or missed the bigger picture, or..."

- failed to prioritise responsibly – we've decided (consciously or unconsciously) that we can't do it, shouldn't do it or simply don't want to, or that someone else will do it, or..."

- failed to act on our priorities – we've been less than Authentic when prioritising and/or we're afraid of acting on our prioritisation and haven't been sufficiently Courageous to overcome that fear.

● ● ●

10

The 'dance' between Responsibility and Authenticity

• ● •

RESPONSIBILITY and Authenticity often come into conflict with one another. When I choose "I can't" or "I don't want to" as reasons for de-prioritising something for which I might otherwise take responsibility, it could well be because I'm being Authentic. I'm accepting my limitations, being true to who I am or prioritising other aspects of my life. When I take on responsibility for another piece of work, project or department that doesn't fit with my personal vision for myself and my career, I'm at risk of failing to self-actualise. When I hold back on some difficult feedback because a team member has just told me his father is dying, you might say I'm being Responsible to him at the expense of being Authentic in the interaction.

> "If I am not for myself, who will be for me? If I am only for myself, what am I?"
>
> Hillel the Elder, Jewish religious leader in the 1st century BCE[118]

Buddhism teaches Four Noble Truths. The essence of these is that everything is always in a state of flux and that our reluctance to accept this is what causes us to feel dissatisfaction. Our own contradictory natures create an internal 'tug of war', pulling us back and forth. We are averse to some objects and experiences and crave others; we want to feel part of a group *and* maintain our individual identities. Getting past this noise and disruption requires attaining a calmness or coolness of mind.

The relationship between Authenticity and Responsibility sometimes feels like that tug of war (see 'Authentically irResponsible' and 'Responsibly inAuthentic')

Authentically irResponsible

Gerald Ratner, former CEO of British jewellery company Ratners Group knocked £500 million off the value of his company in 1991 with the words "People say, 'How can you sell this for such a low price?' I say, 'because it's total crap,'" and by announcing that the company's jewellery was cheaper than "a prawn sandwich but probably wouldn't last as long."[119]

Theresa May, Britain's Home Secretary, appeared on BBC television in 2012 as part of a campaign to convince the British public to monitor their alcohol intake in a bid to improve the health of the nation. When asked how many units she drank a week she said she had no idea.[120]

Responsibly inAuthentic

The heads of Bear Sterns, Enron and RBS all assured the media and their clients, customers and investors that everything was fine when their companies were on the brink of disaster. Why? Maybe because they didn't know. Maybe because they were too scared to admit their mistakes. Or maybe because they have a responsibility to maintain their stakeholders' confidence because falling stocks and a rush on banks only exacerbate the problem.[121]

Japan's Education Ministry amended textbooks to include smaller figures for the casualties inflicted on other Asian countries during World War II because of its long-term responsibility to the Japanese nation's identity.[122]

In the tug of war between being Authentic and being Responsible, we long for ways to balance the two. We judge ourselves for failing to do so. We find ourselves making compromises that we later realise were to the detriment of both. In many respects, this is because we have an unhelpful attitude to balance.

Warren Bennis (who advised four presidents and has been a pioneer of leadership research since the 1960s) characterises this attitude well when he says "*Balance* is an engineering term that means you put the little weights on each side, and if you're really a good person, you'll come out equal. We have to be aware that we swing back and forth. It is choices all the time, not balance."[123]

The British psychiatrist Maurice Nicoll said we often misuse the term "balance", equating it with feeling things less strongly than others do. "To be balanced is not to be stupid," he says, "but to be alive to every side of existence."[124]

I think of the relationship between Authenticity and Responsibility – and Courage – as a *dance*. It's an endless, fluid movement that requires us to invest conscious effort, live in far more than a small part of ourselves and be "alive to every side of existence" rather than drifting through life dispassionately.

There are four mistakes to be made in the dance between the ARC qualities:

1. We can remain static between two points, lacking the mental agility to sprint between them (that Nicoll associates with stupidity and a failure to be truly alive)

2. We can embrace one and not the other(s) – like irresponsibly Authentic Gerald Ratner, and the responsibly inAuthentic leaders at Bear Sterns, Enron and RBS

3. We can confuse one with the other(s) – as I did, mistaking Authenticity for Courage when I was hailed as a hero for my actions during an armed robbery

4. We can try to find a compromise between them, which makes less of both – being a bit Authentic and a bit Responsible doesn't really cut it.

Any of these 'miss-steps' in the dance lessen us and lessen the essence of authenticity and responsibility. The *real* value to be had from authenticity, responsibility *and* courage is to combine them to make something better.

The dance is where the real meat of these three ARC qualities lies; it's there that we find the real challenges and the test of who we are.

When we take on any role – whether it's 'leader', 'parent' or anything else – we take on responsibilities and expectations. Some are imposed by others, some by ourselves. Some are real, some are imagined. Some are fair, some are not. Take a look at your right hand. In it sits the fact that we are all utterly insignificant; in the vastness of the universe, we are specks of dust. Not only that, but our lives are so short that we'll be gone and forgotten in an instant. This is a truth.

Now look at your left hand. This is where another truth sits: most of us are incredibly significant to ourselves and those around us, and we know that one person can make a difference to the lives of millions, and to future generations. In this hand sits the truth that, whatever your belief system, the human body alone is a stunningly impressive thing. The truth that life is precious and a single moment can be incredibly complex, incredibly emotional and meaningful.

There's no halfway house between these two truths: opting for some mid-point between "utterly insignificant" and "stunningly significant" gives us nothing of value. Choosing one hand over the other leaves us too attached or too detached. The only healthy way forward is to 'conjoin' these two. And if we can do something that profound, we should be able to conjoin authenticity and responsibility.

The dance in practice

But what does 'conjoining authenticity and responsibility' mean in practice? One of my favourite answers comes from the Sufi[125] term *adab*, which has a number of meanings, including "having the right presence for the role you are in."[126] It's something I was lacking a few years back when I chose responsibility over authenticity during the 'closing ceremony' of a leadership programme in the mountains just outside Madrid. I was sat at the back of the room with the other coaches, behind a semi-circle of 30 participants, each of whom took their turn to stand up and say a few words about their experience. I'd been coaching five of these people, as a group, almost constantly for three days and when one of them – a fifty-year-old Japanese man – took his turn, he said something so moving that it brought tears to my eyes.

I reacted as I believed any psychologist should: I sat there stoically and, when he sat down, I left my seat and found some privacy to wipe my eyes and take a few deep breaths. Then I returned and acted as though nothing had happened. In repressing my emotions, I was inAuthentic with myself and in my interaction with him. However, by maintaining self-control and professional distance, I was being eminently Responsible. At least that's what I thought at the time. In retrospect, I realise that I took a binary approach to the dance, rather than being simultaneously Authentic and Responsible. In doing so, I failed to be as Responsible as I could have been. He'd publicly shared something profound and, in concealing its impact on me, I'd diminished his experience.

Now, though, I try to keep my *adab* with me. When I get those feelings as a reward for my work, I enjoy them but am not overwhelmed by them. And, at the same time, I'm conscious that I need to let participants know that I'm touched by their experience and our connection.

Bringing responsibility and authenticity together means a leader can be authentically aligned with each member of their team simultaneously, and with the team as an entity in itself.

You'll be doing this dance all the time. If your concern for staff morale has ever caused you to conceal your concerns about the company's future, you've been caught in the dance. And the dance offers far greater opportunities to be the best possible version of ourselves.

In the next chapter, I'll summarise the key themes from Part 3. Then we'll look at six steps to being sustainably Responsible – i.e. Responsible without being overwhelmed. Before we move on, though, I'd recommend you take some time to reflect on what we've covered.

In summary

Sometimes we're Authentic at the expense of being Responsible. Sometimes we're Responsible at the cost of being Authentic. Getting it 'right' isn't about being one at the expense of the other, or compromising on both and producing dissatisfaction and underperformance. Getting it 'right' requires a dance in which we conjoin the two qualities to be authentically Responsible and responsibly Authentic.

• ● •

11

Six steps to being sustainably Responsible

• ● •

THE SUGGESTIONS made here are not rules, they're not compulsory and they don't assume you should be taking responsibility for any specific things, causes or people: there are no specific values being promoted, other than your own.

| Realise | Prioritise | Act |

Step 1: Map the system

Step 2: Realise & Prioritise with Authentic insight

Step 3: Prioritise systemically

Step 4: Master time, don't manage it

Step 5: Prioritise & Act authentically

Step 6: Act courageously

STEP 1: Realise by mapping the system

The table overleaf is intended to help you appreciate the full extent of your current, potentially competing responsibilities at work, home and elsewhere. I'd advise redrawing it on a large sheet of paper, or download the spreadsheet at www.leader-space.com/arc-resources.

This exercise takes time and can initially feel overwhelming, but the more comprehensive your approach, the more hope you have of achieving clarity. If you skip this stage, the concept of responsibility may remain just that – a concept that will hang around and make you feel guilty or over-stretched without making any difference to you or your leadership... Fill in the first five columns in the table – you'll complete the others later.

- *Column 1, "Element":* these are your stakeholders. Cover Personal, Professional and Societal, referring back to Chapter 8 if you need to.

- *Column 2, "What am I currently taking?"* What are the benefits of having each of these people or things in your life?

- *Column 3, "What am I currently contributing?"* What benefits are those people or things receiving from you? If they are demanding something of you but have yet to receive it, you could write that in, but put it in brackets.

- *Column 4, "Balance favours"* When you weigh up the benefits to you and the benefits to them, who is gaining the most? If you gain most, then the balance favours you, so write "me". If the balance favours them, write "them". If it's equal, write "=".

- *Column 5, "What more is needed?"* What else could you give or take to make this a fairer exchange (if it's not already equal)? What more does this element need in order to be the best it can be? You should find it fairly easy to come up with things, even if it's difficult to admit to them.

- *Columns 6, 7 and 8* we'll look at later in this chapter. Please don't fill them in yet.

1. Element*	2. What am I currently taking?	3. What am I currently contributing?	4. Balance favours

5. **What more is needed?**	6. **What's stopping me?**	7. **Overarching goals**	8. **What can I change?**

STEP 2: Realise and Prioritise through Authentic Insight

Some people take on too much responsibility, some take on too little. Some take responsibility for the wrong things, which leaves too little time for more important matters. A prime example is the middle manager who's afraid to delegate so finds himself so distracted by operational details that he lacks sufficient time to attend to strategy, internal marketing, team dynamics or stretch projects that might enhance his career.

> "The ultimate act of personal responsibility at work may be in taking control of our own state of mind."
>
> Daniel Goleman, *Working with Emotional Intelligence*[127]

Authentic Insight helps us understand our relationship with responsibility and what causes us to believe we're Responsible for some things and not others. It also helps us see why we're Prioritising the way we are. George W. Bush is a good example. It has been said[128] that his decision to invade Iraq in response to the attacks on 11th September 2001 was an emotionally charged choice to take responsibility on behalf of several nations – responsibility they were still delivering on over a decade later. Had he had sufficient Authentic Insight, George W. might have seen that his interpretation of the facts was distorted by attitudes he picked up from his father. The previous decade's Persian Gulf War was unfinished business for George Bush Senior, who had been president just eight years before George W. took his place in the White House. Not only had he left Saddam Hussein in power, but Saddam had apparently tried to assassinate him two years after the war had ended.

Authentic Insight means surfacing the subconscious mechanisms that are causing us to take or not take responsibility.

Where Prioritisation is concerned, I've found three things useful for raising Authentic Insight. The first is to classify our reasons for avoiding responsibility using the common reasons covered in Chapter 9.

The second tip is to become familiar with our 'hot buttons' – the things people can say or do that bring out the worst in us. A lot has been written on hot buttons, most of it very useful[129], so I won't go into it here.

The third tool for raising our Authentic Insight with regard to responsibility looks at habits and roles.

Many of us follow habitual patterns when it comes to taking, or not taking, responsibility. Do you think you've ever adopted any of these archetypes?[130]

Hero	Loves taking on the big challenges, which prove how talented he or she is and bring glory, status and more tangible rewards.
Martyr	Is convinced no one cares as much as them. They may fantasise about dying under the strain, but in reality the reward comes from basking in the gratitude and sympathies of others.
Rescuer	Rescues *people*, whereas the Hero is there primarily to rescue the situation and to achieve a task. The rescue can be from practical or emotional difficulties.
Resilient Workhorse	Can take anything. No amount of work is too great. Unlike Heroes, Workhorses don't go seeking the attention, but will accept more and more responsibility simply to prove (to themselves or others) that they can.
Impostor	Is wracked with doubt about his or her capabilities and/or intellect and wonders when the rest of the world will realise how useless the Impostor is. Desperate not to be 'found out', they are typically 'anxious overachievers'.
Faithful Hound	Similar to the Resilient Workhorse, but the motive is to please their 'owner' and receive strokes in return, rather than to prove how durable they are.

QUESTION 1

Which one of these archetypes, if any, is you? And what impact does that have on your perception and prioritisation of your responsibilities?

....

....

....

....

....

....

....

....

....

....

QUESTION 2

Return to the table on page 103 and fill in Column 6, "What's stopping me giving/taking what's needed?" *In doing so, ask yourself:*

- **Which of the imbalances in the table are due to either party's failure to Realise their responsibilities?**

- **Which are failures to Prioritise? And which of the ten reasons in Chapter 9 are driving that failure?**

- **Which of the imbalances are failures to Act on a supposed prioritisation?**

- **If you're the one who is not getting what you need, to what extent are you failing to take responsibility for getting it?**

We'll finish this table later in this chapter. For now, just notice the common patterns in Column 6.

QUESTION 3

How does your approach to these responsibilities reflect what you learned about roles and responsibilities in the first organisation you ever joined – i.e. your family? How appropriate does this feel now that you're an adult? What, if anything, needs to change in your attitude to responsibility?

....

....

....

....

....

....

STEP 3: Prioritise systemically

> "People who embrace complexity, in the world around them and inside themselves, are more likely to succeed at difficult everyday challenges than individuals who try to airbrush away these stubborn realities."
>
> Joseph Badaracco, author of *Leading Quietly*[131]

Most people find at least some of their responsibilities are in conflict with each other.

This complexity is what faced Shirley Silverman, whose story is told by Joseph Badaracco[132]. Silverman was a public health official in Florida in the mid-1990s who opted to take responsibility for tackling the alarmingly high infant mortality rate in her city, apparently caused by drug addiction amongst pregnant women. When the mayor bowed to media pressure and called for all women using drugs during pregnancy to be arrested, Silverman assessed the competing needs and responsibilities of the various stakeholders. She saw that:

- health professionals would prioritise patient care and confidentiality over enforcement

- women would prioritise avoiding arrest over getting treated

- the media would prioritise publishing photos of pregnant women in handcuffs over good news stories

- the mayor and police needed to do *something* about the problem

- the racial profile of the majority of women affected meant any punitive approach would create tension between the administration and black and Latino communities.

Having chosen to take responsibility for saving children's lives, Silverman found she now had to take responsibility for their drug-addicted mothers, the communities they came from, the health professionals who treated them, the city's mayor and police and the media – as well as the relationships between all these stakeholders.

In a world that is increasingly interdependent, it's critical that we find a way to navigate these conflicting forces and adopt a different, more systemic way of thinking about challenges. It means differentiating between those challenges that are puzzles and those that are mysteries. Puzzles are essentially questions with simple, concrete answers. The question may be difficult to answer – e.g. "What's our main competitor's focus for next year?" – but the answers themselves are straightforward. Mysteries are far more complex. Solving mysteries isn't about locating discrete pieces of data: it's about seeing through the data to the themes, inter-relationships and wider context.

The problem of humanity's fairly limited response to global warming isn't a puzzle – it's a mystery. There are so many factors at play. Not only do some people question the existence or causes of global warming, but many of the major players have too much to lose by reducing their impact on the environment (see 'We love global warming').

We love global warming

The melting Arctic holds valuable minerals that couldn't be reached before – including an estimated 30% of the world's undiscovered natural gas and 13% of undiscovered oil. When the ice melts, more and more of this can be brought to market. Canada and Russia are hoping to make the most of new shipping lanes that are emerging, including the Northern Sea Route that follows the Siberian coast and cuts the distance between Europe and Asia by more than a third.[133]

The majority of Westerners are naturally inclined towards puzzle-based thinking, rather than solving mysteries.

It's an approach that has served us well in many respects, otherwise we'd have stopped doing it centuries ago. However, it's an approach that promotes the 'systemiser skew' we saw in Chapter 9 and it ignores the fact that everything that happens in the world happens via the relationships *between* things, not within the things themselves[134].

Getting beyond this approach requires us to do two things: empathise with the 'outsiders' and redefine what's 'good for the community', by which I mean the wide landscape of our inter-connected stakeholders.

Empathising with 'outsiders'

When we're working in complex, shifting systems where the practical and ethical factors are unclear, Authentic Insight into the complexity of our own needs and motivations enables us to better understand those of others. Assuming we and others have simple, one-dimensional, storybook motives will drive us toward simple, one-dimensional solutions – solutions that rarely stick[135].

By way of example, take the people at Barclays who became pariahs over the Libor rate scandal in 2012. In reality, they were swimming in a sea of conflicting responsibilities when they (and others) influenced the inter-bank lending rate. I'm not saying they got their priorities *right*, but I'm certain they felt they were being Responsible to *something* when they made the decisions they did – whether it was Personal, Professional or Societal.

Redefining what is 'good for the community'

Empathising with our various stakeholders helps us understand the rich complexity of the system we're working with, but it can generate an awful lot of information. The critical *next* step is to rise up out of the detail and look for the themes. If we fall into the trap of addressing stakeholders in isolation – our boss, direct reports, customer, client, end user – we create an enormous, unworkable 'to do' list that requires us to disappoint some people. I see this often in teams, where each team member Prioritises the team's responsibility for a different stakeholder group, then competes with their colleagues to ensure their preferred stakeholders' needs are met.

Redefining what is good for the community requires us to:

- think more broadly about which stakeholders constitute the community for which we're Responsible

- build on what we've learned by empathising with them, in order to

- *conjoin* the competing needs of those people and things for which we're Responsible.

The temptation is generally to try to seek a bland compromise, to dilute the conflicts, throw water on them or pretend they don't exist. Conjoining those conflicts typically requires us to shift up a level and identify the higher purpose the competing parties have in common. One common binary example comes from the conflict between serving customers' needs and the needs of your organisation. Often the end result is a compromise that eventually becomes a delicate balance in which either party will threaten to leave if their needs are compromised any further. A more robust solution is to find a way for both parties to take a genuine interest in driving each other's success in a sustainable manner. Then you can step back a little and let them get on with it.

More complex conflicts occur between multiple stakeholders, or in leadership teams where each team member prioritises one cause, whether it's generating profit, efficiency, customer service or staff members' need for security and development. The principle is the same: work out the common overarching goal, then take responsibility for that rather than the mass of subordinate details.

QUESTION 4

Return to the table on page 103 and fill in Column 7, "Overarching goals", phrasing each goal as a question written from that stakeholder's perspective. *For example, if it says in Column 5 that one of your team members needs "More involvement in key decisions, and acknowledgement of their efforts and achievements" you might write "How can I get others to value what I could bring to this organisation?" in Column 7.*

QUESTION 5

Once you've completed Column 7 for all the elements in the table, review the questions and work out which ones overlap with others. As you do so, highlight those questions that overlap by marking them with a number and a plus (+) or minus (-) sign (plus meaning the overlap is complementary, minus meaning it's a conflict). *Examples include:*

- *A common theme among your team members, perhaps around reward, morale or professional development*

- *An external stakeholder whose question is "How can I get more value from this organisation?", which overlaps with the team member who's asking "How can I get others to value what I could bring to this organisation?"*

- *An abstract element like 'culture', whose question is "How can I protect our traditional ways of doing things?" overlaps in a conflicting way with 'current strategy' that is asking "How can we more quickly adapt to stay ahead of the competition?"*

STEP 4: Prioritise and Act by mastering time, not managing it

In 2009, stockbroker and former non-executive chairman of the NASDAQ Bernard Madoff was found guilty of what's considered to be the largest financial fraud in American history, costing investors billions of dollars. In her book, *Wilful Blindness*[136], Margaret Heffernan tells how a fraud investigator named Harry Markopolos tried to warn investors about Madoff. He even worked with a Wall Street journalist named John Wilke for three years on the exposé, but apparently "Wilke never had time to write the story."

Markopolos insists Wilke had all the information he needed so we can take one of two positions here:

a.   Wilke intentionally delayed writing the piece – either because *he* didn't believe he had enough evidence or because he was part of some cover up

b.   Wilke simply had too many other things going on.

You could argue that if Wilke had really wanted to write the necessary article, he'd have made the time to do so. Markopolos puts it down to a simple failure to manage his time.

So much has been written about time management over the years. There are so many blogs, books, magazine articles, videos and courses on the topic that it's clearly a skill we're failing to master. This is a great shame when demands on leaders are only going to increase. It is *never* going to get easier. We need to accept one big truth: if we're not managing our responsibilities in the best way we can, it's not tools, tips and techniques that are the key to turning things around, it's our emotions.

All of the prioritisation decisions we make, particularly those we regret, are driven by our emotions. It comes down to fear and happiness and the pursuit of pleasure and the avoidance of pain. We prioritise yet another deadline over a commitment to family or friends because we're afraid of the consequences of doing otherwise. We prioritise watching our favourite TV programme (or even some stuff we know is awful) over spending that time helping someone who is terminally ill because the former gives us more pleasure and the latter might bring us some pain.

To me, the term 'time management' is unhelpful. Even thinking about it makes me feel uneasy, like I'm fighting a battle against enemy forces. I prefer to think of us 'mastering' our time. We own time. Utterly. All the time we have between the day we're born and the day we die is ours. We feel a sense of responsibility to ourselves and others and we apportion our time accordingly. That's it. It's only by owning our lives that we'll ever feel in control.

Owning our lives requires Authentic Insight. It means questioning the decisions we make when prioritising our responsibilities; questioning the "facts" and emotions driving those decisions; questioning the assumptions and motivations.

QUESTION 6

For the next 24 hours, note down the feelings you experience each time you prioritise one activity over another – the feelings that come before, during and after. Write them down and keep them with you throughout the day. At the end of the day, review what you've written and decide what (if anything) you need to change about the way you Prioritise. *One word or phrase for each can be enough, but try to get to a point where you're noticing three distinct emotions at each of those three points.*

....

....

....

....

....

STEP 5: Prioritise and Act authentically

In 1992, Levi Strauss faced pressure from human rights groups to stop using suppliers who employed child labourers. Rather than simply accepting or rejecting the demands, the company took steps to better understand the system in which it was operating. Its own investigations suggested that if they switched suppliers, the children would lose their jobs and potentially be forced into prostitution. Instead of choosing between two evils, the company took an approach that was entirely consistent with its values, and opted to pay the kids to attend school rather than work. And when the children were perceived to have reached maturity (14 years old in Bangladesh), Levi Strauss re-employed them.[137]

In ARC terms, Levi Strauss prioritised systemically by 'empathising with the community', which included its customers, its suppliers and the children they employed, and human rights groups. The company then made an Authentic decision based on its values: rather than simply abandoning the children to appease the human rights groups, they chose to look after them for the longer term. Was it utterly selfless? No, but it was Authentic and Responsible.

QUESTION 7

Return to the table on page 103 and complete the final column, "What can I change?" For each row in the table, think about the following questions before you answer:

- **What is my ultimate intent in this relationship? Is it healthy? Do I need to redefine it?**

- **What do my values say I should do here?** *(You might find this question easier to answer if you've completed the values exercise in Appendix 1.)*

- **How would the best, most Authentic version of me resolve any imbalance?** *(This will capitalise on the work you did in Part 2 of this book.)*

- **Which of the questions in Column 7 is better addressed by someone else in the table? How can I start that process?**

STEP 6: Act courageously

Often, if we've prioritised a responsibility but have failed to act accordingly, the barrier to action is fear. The antidote to fear is Courage. Ask yourself the following question:

QUESTION 8

What actions in Column 8 will require me to be a little more Courageous than I currently am?

....

....

....

....

....

....

....

....

....

....

In summary

Being more Responsible, in a sustainable way, requires us to improve our ability to Realise, Prioritise and Act on our Personal, Professional and Societal responsibilities. Creating a map of our system helps us see the interdependencies more clearly. Thinking of the whole, not just the parts, helps us Prioritise – as does acting as masters of time, not managers of it. Authenticity helps across the board and Courage is what is needed to turn our intentions into action.

● ● ●

12

Questions and commitments

Thinking further

IF YOU'VE ANSWERED all of the questions in Part 3, you'll have done a lot of work on responsibility. I'd encourage you to consider and discuss the following, too:

You

- In which domains am I most Responsible – personal, professional and societal?

- Given my Authentic aspirations in Part 2, where do I see the greatest scope for being more authentically Responsible?

You and your team (or family)

You can either answer these questions yourself, or use them as discussion points for a team meeting.

- What is our shared endeavour?

- To what extent are we as a team (or family) being Responsible in each of the domains?

- How might we better manage our responsibilities to be the best version of ourselves?

Your organisation

- What are we doing that our staff can see is authentically Responsible?

- How Responsible do we seem to our external stakeholders? If we don't already know, how might we find out? What answers might we expect? What would we do with the information?

Your commitments

- Make one big commitment to yourself (in relation to being Responsible) and write it down.

....

....

- Clarify your commitment:

a. Who else is it important to?

....

b. Why is it important, to you and to them?

....

....

- Go back to those 3 significant people in your life (at work or otherwise) and make this commitment explicitly to them. *(As I said in Chapter 7, you could wait until you've finished the book before you do this, but I strongly suggest you share your commitment before reading on. If you've yet to select them make sure they're people that matter to you, whose opinion you value, who would notice quickly if you strayed from your commitment, and who will be honest with you.)*

● ● ●

PART

4

Courageous

13

What do we mean by 'Courageous'?

● ● ●

DEAN BYASS BUYS and sells antique books and manuscripts. He's an unassuming, shaven-headed man whose leanness suits his penchant for yoga. There's an intellectual clarity and intensity to his eyes and he's a powerhouse of literary references and philosophical ideas.

He's not someone you'd necessarily look at and think "Now there's a man I'd expect to be Courageous."

In 2005, Dean and his wife walked from their house to the local city hospital, "I can cope with anything, as long as it's not stage four," he said to her. He'd been in this situation before, in London in 1994: headed to a meeting, following an initial diagnosis, where an oncologist would tell him just how advanced the cancer they'd discovered was. Back then it had been stage two cancer. But this was a relapse, so stage three was the best they could hope for. "I can cope with anything, as long as it's not stage four."

"So, how bad is it?" he said, once he and Jane were sat with the doctor in front of them.

"I'm afraid it's stage four," the doctor replied. Then he launched into his usual monologue about the ramifications, prognosis and various treatments.

Eventually, the doctor paused. "I know this is a lot for you to take in," he said.

"No, it's not," said Dean. "Because I haven't been listening to a word you've said."

It was a joke he would later be proud of, but the truth was Dean's mind was foggy with fear. He couldn't listen, couldn't think. His brain was in a state of quiet panic – quiet on the outside, at least. What do I do? Can I cope with this? A mass of other questions and sensations were firing in all directions, but all of them inside of him.

And then he felt something growing at his core. A cylindrical column of power solidifying in the centre of his body; a thing he believed was the physical embodiment of courage. Unlike the rest of him, this part was focused; this part was liberating. It told him "I can do this". It didn't take away the fear, but it existed alongside it and he knew in that moment that it was the courage not the fear that would be directing his actions from here on in.

In my research into the nature and psychology of courage, I read and heard some truly astounding stories of what people have done in the face of adversity. I also looked at what the military thinks it means and takes to be Courageous, both on and off the battlefield. I went to Sandhurst to speak to the staff officer responsible for leadership development in the British Army. I spoke to the leader of the Welsh Guard in Afghanistan, who'd been awarded the Distinguished Service Order in 2011 for Courageous leadership in Iraq where he'd led an attack on an Al-Qaeda safe-house armed only with a pistol. To help me understand how military courage translates to the workplace, I spoke to retired officers who'd made the transition into civilian roles, including Anton Horne, who had subsequently taken a job in

"We have monuments for people who have displayed physical courage in war. But where are the monuments to people who said 'no, we won't do this because it's a bad or wrong or unethical decision?'"

Lieutenant Colonel Fred Krawchuk, U.S. Army[138]

121

charge of leadership development in a large public sector organisation and now works for one of the 'Big Four' management consultancies.

In speaking to the military, I was struck by their respect for the Courageous actions of civilians, whether in life-threatening situations or otherwise. They also had a strong focus on 'moral courage', as opposed to the 'physical courage' we tend to associate with people whose jobs entail putting their lives on the line. If we're to understand what it means to be Courageous in the workplace we, too, need to think more broadly.

We tend to overlook the courage that's around us every day. Robert Biswas-Diener, author of *The Courage Quotient*[139], calls this 'Courage Blindness'. Its effect is so pervasive that, when he reached out to 20,000 contacts asking them to nominate Courageous people for a financial prize, fewer than ten responded. Almost half of those replied only to tell him the courage award was a bad idea. When he asked people why they'd not nominated anyone they said they didn't know anyone who was really Courageous.

It's perfectly possible that these people were measuring themselves and their peers against Biswas-Diener himself. After all, he's known as "the Indiana Jones[140] of positive psychology". He's a globe-trotting, hands-on, adventurous researcher who endured the painful initiation rites of East Africa's Maasai tribe in his attempts to understand courage. So, despite his efforts, he may have been contributing to the Courage Blindness around him.

Defining (or redefining) courage

Two thousand years ago, the Chinese Confucian philosopher Mencius argued that we can't develop courage as a society unless we stop equating courage with extreme levels of physical bravery. If we're to raise levels of courage in the workplace we need to recognise that courage isn't (necessarily) about facing physical danger or being a hero in the classic manner of movies, comics and Greek mythology. It's often about small victories, perseverance and being Courageous enough to speak up and challenge the status quo.

Courage, and the lack of it, is contagious. If we recognise the Courageous acts we and others perform daily, then we're more likely to be more Courageous ourselves. Yes, it's Courageous to battle cancer; to try for years to have a child despite ten miscarriages; to bring up two children as a single parent on a low income; to set up a home for battered women. Yes, it's Courageous to blow the whistle on your company's irResponsible accounting practices. It's *also* Courageous to decide *not* to act under pressure to make a decision, or to accept responsibility for something you could dodge if you wanted to. It can take courage to give away the credit for something we could have claimed as our own; to trust an unproven subordinate to take on a task that's out of their comfort zone; to take on a stretching assignment; to challenge the boss, or a client or customer, by saying 'No' or telling them they've got something wrong. We're Courageous when we step into other difficult conversations: firing a member of staff, holding them accountable or giving them particularly negative feedback.

It's Courageous to nurture a direct report whom we know has more potential in the job or organisation than we do; to present an idea or vision that goes against the status quo; to stay focused on that vision when others are losing faith and our creditors are closing in. It requires a certain kind of courage to accept that our own idea might not be the best on offer, or to name the elephant in the room. It takes courage to stop seeing ourselves as victims and accept ownership of our part of the problem so we can take a more adult, proactive role in formulating a solution.

> "[Courage] is an important phenomenon, a vital part of living a full and engaged life, a topic directly relevant to management and business, and a concern that touches literally everyone"
>
> Dr Robert Biswas-Diener, author of *The Courage Quotient*[141]

The common denominator in any Courageous act is that we're acting in spite of our fear. That's why, for me, the best definition of courage comes in the form of 'Feel the fear and do it anyway*', a term coined by Susan Jeffers, PhD[142]. It's a simple definition, one that allows courage to happen anywhere. It's a definition that can apply to individuals, teams and even potentially organisations.

A definition that works across cultures

Like any human behaviour, Courageous acts are the result of an interaction between individuals and their environment, but the psychological mechanism that ultimately determines whether someone takes Courageous action lies within the individual. How someone perceives the threats in a given situation depends in part on their cultural background. Members of some cultures might fear a threat to their family's honour more than the threat of losing a limb.

There are a number of other reasons I believe 'feel the fear and do it anyway' is the best available definition of what it means to be Courageous, regardless of cultural differences. The kind of courage the world needs of its leaders demands that they 'feel the fear and do it anyway'. It also demonstrates why it was more Authentic than Courageous for me to tackle an armed robber when I was seventeen: while it may have *looked* brave from the outside, I felt no fear, therefore it wasn't a Courageous act.

The combined work of Biswas-Diener and fellow positive psychologist Martin Seligman[143] demands that, in order to be Courageous, an action "must be morally desirable, respectable, and lead to laudable results"[144], must "not diminish others" and must make the individual doing it feel good. I disagree – not on moral grounds, but on psychological ones. These extra ingredients blur the distinction between courage and responsibility,

---

* Feel the Fear and Do It Anyway® is the registered trade mark of The Jeffers/Shelmerdine Family Trust and is used with their permission.

or specify a particular *type* of courage rather than helping us understand this quality in its entirety.

As in Parts Two and Three, we'll look at some common barriers to being Courageous and how we can overcome them. We'll also touch three times on the dance between courage and our other two ARC qualities.

First, though, I'd like us to explore what it means to 'feel the fear' and what it is we might 'do anyway'.

Looking at courage in three dimensions

Dean's experience is the epitome of our definition of Courage: there's the fear, the threat, and there's the will to "do it anyway" – which manifested itself in that column of certainty that formed in the core of his body. Importantly, his story also supports Biswas-Diener's findings that the fear and the will to act are driven by two distinct psychological processes operating simultaneously. These processes each have their own web of brain cells and each feed into the pre-frontal cortex[145] – 'the CEO of the brain', where we make our decisions. One, the 'behavioural activation system' (BAS), drives our impulsive, pleasure-seeking behaviours. The other, the 'behavioural inhibition system' (BIS), focuses on worrying, identifying threats and avoiding pain. Essentially, they're acting as accelerator and brake. As Biswas-Diener said in an interview in 2012, "A person's courage quotient... is simply a ratio between these two processes – our 'willingness to act' divided by our fear. If they are equal, or if fear is greater, then a person will not act courageously."[146]

In Dean's case, the BIS fired panicked thoughts and emotions in all directions, the BAS created a column of focus and power at the centre of his body. Sports people feel it too, even (or sometimes especially) when they're playing at a level that's world class. When a professional golfer 'chokes' as they approach the green, or a striker makes a seemingly stupid mistake during a penalty shootout, or a tennis player loses a single point then loses their form for the rest of the game, I believe they're at the mercy of the fear-focused BIS.

It's these two independent systems that give us the first two dimensions of Three-Dimensional Courage™: the type of threat we're facing and the type of action we take in spite of it. The third dimension is the *duration* of the Courageous action.

DURATION Hot			
Enduring			
	THREAT		
ACTION	Mortal	Social	Psychological
Physical			
Moral			
Intellectual			
Aspirational			

Why do we need three dimensions? Two reasons:

1. Understanding the different types of threat helps us better understand what gets in the way of courage in organisations. Understanding the various types of action helps us acknowledge courage in its less glamorous incarnations, thereby reducing Courage Blindness.

2. Previous attempts to categorise types of courage have produced a bewilderingly inconsistent set of lists. I believe a three-dimensional model offers the most coherent answer.

The First Dimension: Types of Threat

When we feel fear, it's because we perceive a threat. There are three types of threat:

1. Mortal threats
Anything that threatens to cause physical pain, damage or death to the person in question.

126

2. Social threats

Far more common in the workplace than mortal threats, these include anything that causes us to believe our relationships with others are at risk – for example, when we fear they might stop liking or respecting us.

In a massive analysis of 208 studies involving 6153 people, two psychologists at the University of California found that we suffer far more when subjected to social threats than we do when the threat is purely physical[147]. When we add an audience to a challenging situation, we increase the stress levels – as you'll know if you've ever done any public speaking.

3. Psychological threats[148]

Anything that threatens our sense of identity, our sanity, spirit, soul or ongoing emotional stability – as opposed to our relationships with others.

The notion of psychological threats allows us to see courage in people's spiritual or religious challenges and their willingness to confront their addictions, phobias and psychological disorders. It also helps us see courage in the manager who was bullied by her boss to the extent that she was signed off with stress, but who took her employer to a tribunal and won, then battled her diminished self-confidence to secure a better job elsewhere.

Of course, whether you or I perceive the same thing as a threat will depend on our personal circumstances. If you're a tiger handler, you'll probably feel less of a mortal threat standing in a cage with a fully-grown tiger than I would. If you're unused to giving formal presentations you'll probably feel a greater social threat than I would if someone asks you to speak to 50 senior managers. Thus, courage is relative.

> "Ask yourself these two questions: If not me, then who? If not now, then when?"
>
> Bill George, *True North*[149]

The Second Dimension: Types of Action

The three types of threat focus on what fear the individual is feeling. The four types of action tell us what they're "doing anyway".

There are two ways to look at this second dimension: the resource the action draws upon and the motivation behind it. Some people also find it helpful to think of these four in terms of hands (or body), heart, mind and spirit.

TYPE OF ACTION	RESOURCE	MOTIVATION	FOCUS
Physical	Body	Physically defeat the opposition	Hands
Moral	Sense of right and wrong	Do what is morally right	Heart
Intellectual	Intellect	Do what is logically the best thing	Mind
Aspirational	Sense of own or others' potential	Be the best I/we can be	Spirit

Looking at Courageous events in these two dimensions (the type of threat and the type of action) enables us to categorise a wide range of Courageous acts. We see Dean's as a physical reaction in the face of a mortal threat (cancer); whistle-blowers taking a moral stand at the risk of social ostracism or bodily harm; team members championing an unpopular idea in the face of ridicule, or despite the idea challenging their own world view. So let's look closer at these four types of Courageous action.

1. Physical Courage

Dean Byass demonstrated physical courage in the face of a mortal threat. When he heard that his cancer had reached stage 4, he felt his body *literally* react to the diagnosis, mobilising its resources in response to the fear swelling within him. Unlike some cancer patients, he's adamant that his courage had nothing to do with being strong for his family and friends, nothing to do with his aspirations for himself or for them. It was purely physical – an animal urge to defeat the opposition. In Dean's case, the opposition was cancer. On the battlefield, the opposition might be enemy troops.

These are examples of physical courage in the face of a mortal threat – using our bodies to respond to a threat to the body itself. In 21st-century middle-class Britain and similar cultures, this is by far the most acceptable use of physical courage. It's generally not acceptable to respond physically to a social or psychological threat. For instance, in most (but not all) modern workplaces, it's unacceptable for me to punch one of my colleagues because his politicking has undermined my reputation and self-esteem; however, 200 years ago I could have challenged him to a duel.

2. Moral Courage

In the 1950s, Field-Marshall Slim described moral courage as "a more reasoning attitude [than physical Courage] that enables a man coolly to stake career, happiness, his whole future on his judgement of what he thinks either right or worthwhile."[150]

Many of the tales of courage I read and heard in the course of my research were cited as examples of physical courage but actually had moral courage at their heart. The confusion comes from the fact that these are instances of moral courage in the face of mortal threats – similar to the courage shown by Ghandi, Mandela and Martin Luther King, all of whom stood up for what they believed to be right, despite threats of pain and death.

In most organisations, though, moral courage takes place in the face of social and psychological threats, rather than mortal ones. The majority of whistle-blowers fear for their jobs and career prospects, not for their lives. People's failures to report incidents of child abuse by Irish Catholic priests were primarily driven by their fear of upsetting the social status quo or being branded a liar. The abused may have feared for their safety, but also suffered the same social threats and the psychological threat of being forced to redefine themselves as objects of abuse, rather than love. When staff at BP, Transocean and Halliburton failed to stand up to the cost-cutting practices that contributed to the Deepwater Horizon disaster in the Gulf of Mexico, it was likely to be social pressure from stakeholders that prevented them demonstrating moral courage.

This focus on doing what is morally right is closely linked with integrity, authenticity and responsibility. What we consider "morally right" will depend, to some extent, on our values and our sense of responsibility. However, there do seem to be some universal moral instincts, irrespective of culture and whether people subscribe to any particular religion or none at all[151].

3. Intellectual Courage

Intellectual courage is the cognitive 'head', where moral courage is the values-driven 'heart'. It's something that's lacking in existing theories of Authentic and Ethical Leadership, but does feature in the equally popular model of 'Transformational Leadership', which calls on us to stimulate ourselves and those we lead "to question assumptions, reframe problems, and approach old situations in completely new ways."[152] Intellectual courage is about doing what is intellectually right, getting at the right answer, the objective truth.

There are five key ways I've seen people demonstrate intellectual Courage:

1. Taking a radical, innovative position; raising an issue that everyone else is afraid to name (the 'elephant in the room' or 'rotting elk'); pointing out flaws in a proposal that everyone seems to think is flawless

2. Admitting we're wrong or don't know the answer

3. Unlearning old mind-sets and old ways of doing things

4. Holding a paradox without resolving it. Paradox is an ever-present ingredient of leadership decision-making. Do we focus on strategy or operational issues? Tasks or people? Innovation or commoditisation? Profit or sales? Our clients or our staff? Do we ask our people what they think we should do or earn our salaries by telling them?

5. Embracing ambiguity and complexity.

The concept of complexity is often misunderstood so I'd like to touch on that now. Fixing a jet engine is a complicated task, but each component has a fixed, clear role and behaves predictably. Bringing up a child is complex: the child exists in a shifting system (school, friends, family, media, etc.); the child, too, is constantly changing.

When we're leading people and organisations, the majority of the challenges we face are complex and it can be overwhelming. All too often, leaders and leadership teams respond by assuming or pretending their problems are less complex than they are. Faced with a problem with a complexity Level of 5, they assume it's only Level 3 so they launch a Level 3 solution.

You might be wondering what I mean by Level 5 and Level 3. To understand the underlying *concept* of levels, I'd encourage you to imagine your way through the 'Levels of Complexity' panel below.

Levels of complexity[153]

Imagine you're four years old again, standing at the top of some enormously tall building, looking down at the streets below.

"Look at the tiny people," you say.

Now, you're nine years old, visiting the same spot, seeing things differently.

"Look how small the people look," you say. Your eyes are the same. The scene is the same. But now you're able to look at the *process* of seeing. You're able to look at your own *perception* of the scene and comment on the distortion. You have gone up a level in the complexity of your thinking.

In thinking about this situation as you read this book, you've moved up another level. You're thinking about the process of *examining* your own perceptions – your *perception* of a perception.

Each time we move up a level, we're able to look at the lenses through which we were previously looking.

On a practical level, I find it helpful to distinguish two broad levels of complexity, as suggested by the authors of *The Practice of Adaptive Leadership*[154]: problems are either 'technical' or 'adaptive' – the latter being the more complex of the two. A technical problem is clearly defined and the solution is clear, too, although it might be complicated.

An adaptive problem is one where the solution requires some significant learning on the part of those involved. Not only that, but the diagnosis of the problem (even the very definition of the problem) requires further learning.

The ability to work with adaptive challenges, or move up through levels of complexity, isn't a matter of IQ. Our cognitive intelligence is actually more relevant when we're faced with technical challenges. Adaptive challenges require us to understand the cognitive and emotional constraints of the system that's facing the problem, to gauge the extent to which the problem takes us beyond our current 'mental map'. In doing so, we need to challenge our assumptions, question our understanding of the situation, the system, even the way the world works.

The more we challenge our own fundamental assumptions and beliefs, the greater the psychological threat. The more we challenge those of others, the greater the risk that they'll fight back by rejecting or persecuting us – a social threat to add to the psychological one. It takes intellectual courage to pursue the truth in the face of these threats.

4. Aspirational Courage

Aspirational courage is driven by our sense of our own or others' potential – an ambition of sorts, to be the best I or we can be. This isn't just about career aspirations, it includes the Courageous pursuit of self-actualisation. And, for those who have managed to combine being Authentic with being Responsible, aspirational courage is what helps them work towards 'self-transcendence' – a less selfish form of self-actualisation which focuses on being the best contributor I can be, by wisely investing my privileges.

It's Aspirational courage that enables an entrepreneur to start a small business in the slums of Bangkok or Calcutta that becomes a beacon for locals and investors and eventually turns the entrepreneur into a national icon. It's this form of courage that was shown by a woman determined to have a family despite having ten miscarriages in ten years – threatening her physically and psychologically, and putting her at grave risk of others ostracising her for her choices. And my friend who was paralysed in an accident and has subsequently re-educated and reinvented himself as a positive force for others. And our friends with terminal illnesses who know they've lost the battle but aspire to die with dignity.

Achieving our ambitions – whether they're professional or personal – almost always comes at a price. In these days of entitlement, we can download music, video and books for free in an instant; we have access to more information than we could possibly digest; in many countries we're allowed to vote and can get any food we like with minimal fuss, cheaper than it probably should be. It's easy to think we can have it all.

We see celebrities and sporting stars explode onto our screens but rarely see the effort it took to get that one big break. Perhaps the same is true of many CEOs, Managing Directors, Partners and Ministers. We don't see the effort it took to get there. Very few stellar performers manage to fulfil their potential without the courage to give something up along the way. Maybe they've missed critical moments with their kids. Maybe their friends haven't seen them for months. Maybe they've made some enemies along the way. Maybe they've not had as much fun as they might have done, or feel they're lacking fulfilment in other ways. Once again, we're faced with the tension between the three ARC qualities. Here, being Courageous can come at the price of being truly Responsible. The key, as always, lies in managing those tensions in the healthiest way possible.

The third dimension: Duration

In the 1950s, British physician Alice Stewart set out to find the cause of a marked increase in the number of childhood deaths from leukaemia[155].

Only one organisation was sufficiently interested to give her any funding. Even they only gave her enough to cover her travel expenses.

Hoping to gather data from all mothers whose children had died of leukaemia in a three-year period, Alice designed an interview script and took it personally to the medical officers of 203 health departments. This itself was quite some achievement, given her commitments as a divorced mother of two. In terms of Three Dimensional Courage, she demonstrated aspirational and moral courage in the face of significant social threats.

Alice was very persuasive. Many of those 203 health departments agreed to use their own people to conduct the research on her behalf. They surveyed 2000 people, helping Alice link incidents of cancer to children's exposure to x-rays while still in the womb. She published her findings in 1956, but displayed intellectual courage in continuing to question her conclusions – even though many people already believed she'd earned a Nobel prize. She kept gathering data, eventually concluding that a child a week was dying in the UK because of the practice of X-raying pregnant women.

The medical establishment was so in love with X-rays that it lacked the intellectual and moral courage to question their use. It took 24 years for American hospitals to act on Alice's findings, despite the fact that they were confirmed by independent research. Health professionals in her native UK were even slower. In the hope of discrediting her, some even published research of their own that they knew was flawed, and Alice's main detractor, whom she knew personally, didn't recant until the 1990s – when Alice was in her late 80s.

1. Enduring Courage

Alice Stewart's story demonstrates enduring Courage, which is synonymous with words like 'tenacity' and 'perseverance'. As Joseph Badaracco says, leadership in a civilian setting is most often "a long, hard race, run on obscure pathways, not a thrilling sprint before a cheering crowd."[156] It's this enduring courage that puts an athlete on the podium, raises an entrepreneur out of the slums of Mumbai or helps him establish the first commercial space flight. It's this long-term courage that leaders in corporations and government departments need in order to persist with significant organisational change programmes.

2. Hot Courage

Hot courage is quick and immediate. It's the kind of courage that spurs people to save children from burning buildings and swollen rivers, or to storm an enemy position. It's the kind of courage that has us taking a stand in a single business meeting as opposed to persisting with a position for weeks, months or years.

So, Courage is best seen in three dimensions: the nature of the threat we're facing, the thing we do in spite of it, and the length of time for which courage is demanded of us. Courage also works best when combined with our other two ARC qualities, so it's to this dance that we'll turn our attention in Chapter 14. First, though, I encourage you to answer the following questions...

QUESTION 1
Write down three situations in which you believe you demonstrated courage. For each, record the threat, the action and whether the courage required of you was 'hot' or 'enduring'.

QUESTION 2

Consider two situations when you showed a lack of courage.

a. **In each of them, what type of action was required?** *(i.e. what would you have done had you been more Courageous at the time?)*

....

....

....

....

....

....

b. **What was the nature of the threat?**

....

....

....

....

c. **If you faced these situations again, what would you do differently?**

....

....

....

....

....

QUESTION 3

What is the biggest challenge you're facing at work right now? *(If you can't think of anything, ask yourself "What is the biggest challenge I'm likely to face in the next six months?")*

....

....

....

....

....

a. **What are the threats that make it hard for you to step up to this challenge?**

....

....

....

b. **What type/types of action is/are required of you to address this challenge?**

....

....

....

....

In summary

Many of us only associate courage with extreme acts of physical bravery. This blinds us to the many varied examples of people being Courageous in the workplace. Courage and the lack of it are contagious.

If we're to fully appreciate what it means to be Courageous, it helps to see courage in three dimensions:

DURATION			
Hot			
Enduring			
	THREAT		
ACTION	Mortal	Social	Psychological
Physical			
Moral			
Intellectual			
Aspirational			

1. The nature of the threat (real or perceived) that provokes the fear

   - Mortal threats are dangers to the body

   - Social threats are those that provoke fear about our relationships with others

   - Psychological threats are threats to our sanity, spirit, soul or emotional stability

2. The kind of action we take in spite of it: physical, moral, intellectual or aspirational

3. The duration of that Courageous action – whether it's quick and Hot, or long and Enduring.

● ● ●

14

Courage is key to Authenticity and Responsibility

● ● ●

CHURCHILL'S WORDS

echo those of the early philosophers. In Greece, great thinkers like Aristotle and Plato believed courage to be one of four cardinal virtues – with justice, temperance and prudence – and that it could be perfected only in relation to the other three[158].

We've already seen that fear is one of the key obstacles to being Authentic and to being Responsible. The role of courage in consistently manifesting those two qualities is clear in our definition of courage itself: 'feel the fear and do it anyway'. As Biswas-Diener says, courage makes us "better able to live a full and virtuous life... more likely to face challenges with grace, connect with and inspire others, and be a force for good."[159]

Courage feeds Authentic Insight and Intent

It takes courage to dig around in ourselves, to peel back the many layers of our psychological onion but, if we fail to do so, we fail to understand the drivers behind many of our decisions as leaders. Maybe, like me, your desire to succeed is rooted in your need to make a dead parent proud of you and leave something tangible behind where he left nothing but his children, a devastated wife and a house she couldn't afford to maintain. Maybe your preference for cost-cutting over investment is due to your parents working four jobs between them to support a family. Maybe your relationship with your staff or your boss is rooted in the patterns you formed as a child.

Peeling the onion

The Chief Executive Officer was a very tall, robustly built and somewhat red-faced man in his last role prior to retirement. He was a real, palpable presence in the room and was clearly senior to everyone present – as opposed to some CEOs who are more collegiate with their fellow board members. The Finance Director was of similar height, 15-20 years younger and seen as a strong candidate for the CEO job once the seat was vacated. To the other board members he was a classic alpha male, but to the CEO he was little more than an affectionate puppy. Why? Because the FD desperately craved the CEO's approval. Why? Because his father had never given it to him.

Understanding this was critical to changing a destructive dynamic that eroded the other directors' faith in the FD. It took a fair amount of courage for the FD to confront those 'demons' and exorcise them.

It takes courage to be honest about our values – to check our stated priorities against our actions. As the authors of *Adaptive Leadership* say "You know best who you really are by watching what you do rather than listening to what you say."[160]

Without Courage, we shy away from being honest with ourselves. We might avoid introspection altogether or, worse, adopt a 'holier than thou' approach where we focus on the flaws of others. We humans have a natural tendency to blame others' failings on fundamental flaws of character and our own on the situation around us. Doing so enables us to lower our own and others' expectations of us and our leadership. So we counter tales of authenticity, responsibility and courage with evidence that the people involved are far from perfect. It's easy: John F. Kennedy cheated on his wife; Churchill drank too much; Gandhi was troubled by depression; Mandela "craved the company of celebrities", was "a rabble-rouser in his youth" and failed to stand up to his political colleagues on important issues like AIDS and Zimbabwe[161].

Courage makes for more Authentic Interactions

Remember the fears we identified in Chapter 5 that get in the way of being Authentic with others?

If we give in to those fears, we focus on protecting ourselves and avoiding the openness and vulnerability that's essential for true connections with others. At our worst, we become suspicious, paranoid. We see malice and attacks in the smallest actions of others. We cover ourselves in armour plating, a cocoon, or mask of invulnerability – all of which undermines our efforts to gain the trust of others.

Research on populations as diverse as doctors[162], married couples[163] and teenagers[164] has shown that the daily practice of courage helps us be more Authentic and makes our relationships more rewarding. The classic Prisoners' Dilemma demonstrates the power of courage in promoting authenticity.

The dilemma is highly representative of the interpersonal 'games' we play at work. In reality, the 'game' plays out in a number of 'rounds' – not just the single round of our decision in our respective prison cells.

The Prisoners' Dilemma

This game is run in laboratories and training rooms across the world. You and I are 'arrested' for a crime we committed together – a crime that carries a ten-year prison sentence. The Police lack the evidence they need to convict us for this crime, but they have enough to imprison us for a lesser offence, with a two-year sentence. They offer me a deal: if I give them enough evidence to convict you, they'll let me go free.

They offer you exactly the same deal. However, if *both* of us provide evidence against the other, we'll be sentenced to five years in jail.

What do you do?

If you and I are faced with the Prisoners' Dilemma, there are two strategies you could adopt: either you prey on me, or you trust in my good nature not to prey on you. I, too, have to choose one of those two strategies. Statistically speaking, where there are a number of 'rounds', the optimal approach is to trust first – that is, to be Authentic and Responsible – and then, in the second round, to do whatever the other person did in the last round[165].

Trusting first is an act of courage. But, if the other party took advantage of you in the first round, it takes even greater courage to trust again in the second. Statistically speaking, trusting again if you've been 'betrayed' is not the best option. However, it does demonstrate commitment to being Authentic and Responsible. Being Courageous means being Authentic and Responsible even if others fail to immediately reciprocate, even if it costs us in the short term. As a leader, you are a role model, and good role models don't just do the 'right thing' once, then cave in and do whatever's easiest.

QUESTION 4

Take the following task, based on the work of Chris Argyris[166], to your next two meetings…

Draw a line down the centre of a sheet of paper. In the left hand column, write down what you say in that meeting (a brief summary will do), and in the right hand column write down what you were really thinking at the time.

What does the difference between the two columns tell you about your courage (and authenticity) in that meeting?

Courage facilitates Authentic Action

"The world may have very different expectations for you and your leadership than you have for yourself... you will be pressured by external forces to respond to their needs and seduced by rewards for fulfilling those needs. These pressures and seductions may cause you to detour from your True North... It requires courage and resolve to resist the constant pressures and expectations confronting you and to take corrective action where necessary."

Bill George, *True North*[167]

Bill George was CEO, then chairman of the world's leading medical technology company from 1991 to 2002; the company's market capitalisation averaged 35% growth per year. He's been on the board at ExxonMobil, Goldman Sachs and Novartis and has taught leadership at Harvard Business School since 2004. He's been hailed as Executive of the Year, Director of the Year and one of the top 25 business leaders of the past 25 years. He's also involved with numerous global programmes aimed at bringing health and peace to the world.

With co-author Peter Sims – who was once part of Deloitte Touche Tomatsu's Global Strategy Team – Bill George interviewed 125 leaders aged 23 to 93. The one criterion for being interviewed was that they have a reputation for being Authentic.

Every single one of these 125 leaders needed courage to earn and live up to that reputation. It's only through courageously demonstrating responsibly Authentic Action in the face of adversity that we demonstrate our integrity – a quality that was rated the most desirable attribute in a leader (by a long way) in a survey of around 54,000 people[168].

George and Sims state that "You do not know what your true values are until they are tested under pressure." I believe they're oversimplifying things; I believe it's perfectly possible to have an accurately ranked list of my top 5 values and still fail to act in accordance with them under extreme pressure.

There are times when we *want* to act in a certain way, times when we know what the Authentic Action would be, but we lack the courage to do it. Re-prioritising our values after the stressful event, to explain our actions on that occasion, *can* be the right thing to do: it can bring us closer to an Authentic understanding of ourselves. But it can also be the wrong thing to do: it can rob us of our aspirations to be the best version of ourselves that we can be.

This aspiration to be the best we can be brings us back to self-actualisation. Unfortunately, as the Jesuit priest and psychotherapist Anthony De Mello wrote in his book *Awareness*, "People don't live, most of you, you don't live, you're just keeping the body alive."[169] I see this all too often in the course of my work: people whose jobs or careers are a necessary evil to them, who seem painfully unaware that "we live in a flash of light; evening comes and it is night forever."[170] It reminds me of the following passage, from a novel I once read:

"...the work that people did had been broken down into jobs that were the same every day, in organizations where people were interchangeable parts. All of the story had been bled out of their lives. That was how it had to be; it was how you got a productive economy... If [people] came home at day's end with interesting stories to tell, it meant that something had gone wrong: a blackout, a strike, a spree killing... [People] had to look somewhere outside of work for a feeling that they were part of a story… Something with a beginning, middle, and end in which you played a significant part"[171]

Leadership is one of life's greatest opportunities for truly living, for authoring our own stories and helping others write their own. But it takes courage to take the pen from those who might write our story for us and do the work ourselves. This isn't about quitting our jobs to devote our lives to the pursuit of world peace. If everyone who wants to 'do good' takes that path, the less "worthy" occupations and organisations that keep our economies going will be left to the hands of leaders and staff who are morally bankrupt. Courageous self-actualisation means being conscious and proactive in our day-to-day choices – being the best we can be in the environment we're in. At the simplest level, it's as basic as letting ourselves be happier – the failure to do so being Number 5 in Bronnie Ware's *Top Five Regrets of the Dying*. "Many [terminally ill patients] did not realise until the end that happiness is a choice," she says. "Fear of change had them pretending to others, and to their selves [sic], that they were content, when deep within, they longed to laugh properly and have silliness in their life again."[172]

QUESTION 5

Complete the following sentence with as many endings as possible… **"If I had no fear, I would…"**[173]

Courage promotes responsibility

When we're afraid, we tend to resist responsibility. We grow childish in our actions and attitudes, avoiding the grown-up work of being in charge and being held accountable. We turn inwards to protect ourselves, just as large numbers of people withdraw funds from a country's banks when the economy takes a turn for the worse – and, in prioritising their own needs over their Societal responsibilities, they cripple the banks and the nations that rush to their aid.

Courage helps us stand our ground – to do what is right, or support the greater good – even when it causes us pain, or delays or prevents us from fulfilling our own ambitions. Ultimately that's what great leadership requires: engaging others with a collective endeavour that is bigger than ourselves and bigger than the people we are leading.

I see the dance of courage and responsibility in most boardrooms. For example, I once coached a board of executives who admitted they'd lacked the courage to do the Responsible thing when their country's economy went into recession in 2008. They'd been unwilling to take the tough decisions they all knew were necessary. They'd failed to reduce their headcount and failed to address performance issues – including, frankly, their own failure to take proper responsibility as a board.

So, being Courageous helps us be more Authentic and Responsible. As we saw in Part One of this book, courage also has its own independent role to play in leadership. But, if courage is so fantastic – for leaders and the people and organisations we lead – why don't we see more of it in organisational life? It's not just fear that gets in the way. As we'll see in the following chapter, there are other forces in and around us that can make being Courageous really difficult.

In summary

It takes courage to be Authentic when authenticity comes at a price. Digging deeply into ourselves in pursuit of Authentic Insight can be tough, as can acting in accordance with our values and Authentic Intent. Being open with others, trusting them, striving for self-actualisation: all three can be risky and all might come at a price.

There's a price, too, to being Responsible: we might feel less Authentic; we might need to overcome our own biases or failings; we might need to be Courageous to choose between competing responsibilities.

● ● ●

15

Why it's hard
to be Courageous

• ● •

IN 1989, CONSULTANT anaesthetist Steve Bolsin[174] started work at the Bristol Royal Infirmary, a large British teaching hospital founded in 1735. Mortality rates for children undergoing heart surgery stood at an alarming 30% but the hospital's leadership refused to investigate the surgeons responsible.

Steve wasn't sure how to respond to the situation, prompting some heated discussions with his wife, Maggie – one of which their five-year-old daughter Natasha overheard.[175]

"Natasha came downstairs in her nightgown and asked what we were arguing about," he remembers. "Maggie said: 'Too many kids are dying and Dad doesn't know what to do.' She just looked at me and said: 'You have to stop them killing the children.'"

Steve says of that moment: "It was quite obvious to a five year old that it was thoroughly reprehensible behaviour... It is not morally acceptable to experiment on children."

Why is it that 85% of MBA students say they have (on at least one occasion) felt unable to raise an issue or concern to their bosses even though they felt the issue was important[176]? Why is it that investigations of the sinking of the *Herald of Free Enterprise*, the collapse of Enron and the UK's Clapham rail crash all showed that staff in the respective organisations had lacked the moral courage to act on their awareness of risks and malpractice? Why is it that a five-year-old child in Bristol in

1989 seemed more clear about the moral imperative than her father, an experienced medical professional?

Why is it that so many leaders I've worked with have clung to beliefs and ways of operating that are so clearly defunct, despite losing market share and haemorrhaging profits and talented people? Why is it that they defer to people they know are wrong, invest time and energy in projects they know add no value, knowingly delegate to exactly the wrong person, avoid the conversations they know they need to have? Why do 80% of executive teams fail to hold themselves and their staff accountable[177]?

The obvious answer is that they're afraid of the social, psychological and sometimes physical threats in our model of Three Dimensional Courage. However, we know from our definition of courage ('feel the fear and do it anyway') that some people act in spite of that fear. So, what is it that stops us 'doing it anyway'? I see six clear reasons.

1. Because fear works

Fear is a fundamental instinct that keeps us and other animals alive. You might say Egyptian President Anwar El Sadat and Israeli Prime Minister Yitzhak Rabin died because of their courage – both were Courageous and both were assassinated by their own people. In the US, as many as 30% of whistle-blowers were removed from their own offices by armed security guards. Some were left so afraid that they've felt the need to carry a gun.[178] Steve Bolsin and his family faced a range of social and psychological threats following the scandal at Bristol's Royal Infirmary, forcing them to relocate to Australia.

Attitudes to whistle-blowing vary across organisations and cultures, but a 2011 survey suggests that, in the USA at least, retaliation against employee whistle-blowers is on the increase: 22% of staff who had reported misconduct said they experienced some form of retaliation in return. In 2007 it was 12%.[179]

Our brains treat these social and psychological threats in much the same way as the mortal ones, and with good reason. A wealth of studies in humans and other animals show that social status affects health, even when you control for the effects of lifestyle factors like diet and smoking[180], and that the strength of our social bonds with others affects our chances of recovering from diseases like cancer[181]. Without fear, we'd be dead, devoured, destitute or all of the above. That's why courage is so powerful. It's our act of resistance against one of our primal, animal instincts. It's what gives us power over our environment. It's what makes us worthy of free will. After all, what is free will without the courage to use it?

2. Because of our breeding

Our attitudes to fear and courage are generally formed when we're young. We're taught to value certain things, too – wealth, security, status, competence, material things, friendship, freedom and so on. If we learn to value them enough, the fear of losing them can be overwhelming.

Gender plays a part, too. In most 21st-century cultures, males are expected to demonstrate greater physical courage. Males and females are pushed, whether through upbringing or biology, towards different aspirations.

The lessons we teach about fear and courage also vary by country. It's important to remember that there is greater diversity in personalities *within* any given culture than there is *between* cultures, but it's inescapable that the culture in which we're born will have an influence on our attitudes as we grow up. For instance, "in Europe, what Americans see as optimism can simply seem like arrogance."[182]

There are a number of ways to explain the differences. Firstly, according to Dutchman Geert Hofstede, cultures vary in the extent to which they prefer to avoid uncertainty, ambiguity and change[183]. Our culture's desire for 'uncertainty avoidance' will affect our own, and with it our perceptions of what constitutes a threat and what degree of uncertainty warrants a fear response.

Secondly, the more collectivist a culture is, the more modest people tend to be about their capabilities.[184] Relative to their individualistic counterparts, collectivist cultures also tend to emphasise hard work over self-belief, which perhaps explains Dr Fontaine's observation that many Asians prefer to say "This is a very difficult challenge, and I'm trying, even though I may not be able to do it," rather than "I know I can do it, I know I'm good." Arguably, the former is the more Courageous position.

In individualist cultures, the 'can do attitude' is more likely to manifest in an individualist way – in the belief that *I* can overcome a given challenge or that things will go well for *me*. In a collectivist culture, my optimism is a *combination* of belief in myself and belief in the capabilities of the group to which I belong.[185]

One way to look at how courage manifests differently in different cultures is through the lens of our three ARC qualities. For instance, we might say that – compared to Americans – European parents train their children to mix a heavier dose of authenticity into their Courage, tempering it with a level of introspection and humility that Americans might call 'defeatism' or 'false modesty'. We could also argue that, in at least some parts of Asia, courage is mixed with a heavier dose of responsibility than in other countries.

QUESTION 6

When you were a child and teenager, what did your parents, teachers and other role models teach about fear, courage and persistence?

....

....

....

....

....

....

3. Because we don't think straight

As human beings, our thinking and decision-making is subject to a bewildering array of biases that make for illogical outcomes. Two biases are particularly good at nudging us towards the less Courageous path:[186]

Hyperbolic discounting (or 'future discounting')

We typically value the present more than the future. That's why so many people fail to save adequately for retirement and smoke today despite knowing the risks to their future health. It'll sometimes be future discounting at work when leaders put off a difficult but necessary conversation at work, and in leadership teams who refuse to accept the ugly truth that the company needs to reduce headcount or fire one of its clients. They hope their 'future selves' will have the courage to deal with the consequences.

The "licence to sin"[187] effect

Acting courageously can also make us less likely to respond courageously to the next challenge. One reason, as we'll see in Chapter 17, is because it draws on our reserves of courage. Another is because acting courageously can leave us feeling that we've earned the right to be less Courageous next time. Psychologists call this 'moral licensing'. It's based on the premise that we aspire to be morally 'good enough', rather than perfect.

4. Because a lack of courage is contagious

Courage is contagious. Generally speaking, if one person shows courage it *en*courages others. As psychologist Jonathan Haidt at the Stern School of Business confirms, people who witness other people's courage often experience a feeling of elevation and can be inspired to be Courageous themselves[188].

Unfortunately, lack of courage is also contagious. One person's emotional response can determine the mood of the whole group[189].

We saw a lack of moral courage spreading at Abu Ghraib and Camp Breadbasket. We see it in crowds of sports fans who suddenly go on the rampage. We see it in teams and organisations that fail to tackle the few bad apples in their midst and consequently go the way of Enron, Lehman Brothers and Andersen.

5. Because we're trying to be Responsible

Just as authenticity and responsibility sometimes pull against each other, so they sometimes pull against courage. We need to be Courageous without being irResponsible. Otherwise, we risk seeking crushing victories at the expense of ongoing relationships, or forcing our opponents into a corner, making them more resistant and thus creating stronger opposition.

Every organisation has its share of people who are irresponsible, but for every risk-addicted psychopath in the workplace there are at least eight or nine people who could be more Courageous. I'm not talking about headline-grabbing brave. I'm talking about day-to-day Courageous. Sometimes, though, our courage is stifled by our sense of responsibility for the needs or short-term safety of others – our team, for instance, or our business unit, organisation or relationship with a customer.

In balancing responsibility and courage, Joseph Badaracco calls for leaders to take "the rules" very seriously, to understand them and their full moral weight, and to look hard for room to manoeuvre – that is, taking them seriously but bending (never breaking) them. It's important, he says, not to see rules as made to be broken but to "approach ethical problems as entrepreneurs, not clerks".[190] I would put it this way: when you feel the temptation to be less than Courageous, ask yourself…

"Is it responsibility or *fear* that is driving my decision not to be Courageous?"

In Bronnie Ware's *Top Five Regrets of the Dying*[191] it's clear that a lot of people regretted letting responsibility drive them towards a lack of courage and authenticity. "Many people suppressed their feelings in order to keep peace with others," she says. "They settled for a mediocre existence and never became who they were truly capable of becoming. Many developed illnesses relating to the bitterness and resentment they carried as a result."

The most common regret of all, though, was "I wish I'd had the courage to live a life true to myself, not the life others expected of me." Ware writes. "When people realise that their life is almost over and look back clearly on it, it is easy to see how many dreams have gone unfulfilled. Health brings a freedom very few realise, until they no longer have it."

It's not always easy reconciling responsibility and courage. I find some guidance in the expression "Live each day as if it's your last, but tend your garden like you're going to live forever."[192]

6. Because we're trying to be Authentic

As we'll see later, authenticity can be great fuel for courage. However, it can also get in the way. Sometimes our current "honest" appraisal of ourselves and our capabilities is enough to cripple our aspirations or prevent us from doing what's "right".

I've already argued that when I tackled an armed robber it was authenticity not courage that drove me. Let's imagine I *did* see his knife. If I'd had time to engage in Authentic Insight, I might have questioned the reasons I felt compelled to run at the robber and not at the door; some dark primordial impulse, perhaps, driving me into the afterlife in search of my father, who had died when I was a child. Had I had time, I might have done an Authentic appraisal of myself and my role in the situation: a teenage boy with his whole life ahead of him, whose hourly wage was less than the cost of three Sunday newspapers, and who was about to risk his life for a handful of banknotes that would be covered by his multinational employer's insurance policy.

Authentically focusing on ourselves, who we are and how we're feeling can cause us to lose our impetus. When we acknowledge our weaknesses, we risk reducing our confidence; similarly, there's a chance that in trying to be Authentic in our interactions with others we become *too* sympathetic to those we might upset by taking a Courageous decision.

In summary

There are six common reasons why we sometimes fail to be Courageous:

1. Fear is a fundamental instinct that keeps us alive

2. The way each of us was brought up increases our sensitivity to particular threats and affects our attitude to certain types of Courageous action

3. Humans are naturally predisposed to certain cognitive biases that work against Courageous action

4. The lack of courage we see around us is contagious

5. The pressure to be Responsible can hold us back

6. Authentic Insight can affect our perception of the threat and the resources we have to deal with it.

• ● •

16

Reducing the fear

• ● •

THE IMPORTANT QUESTION, where this book is concerned, is: "Can we learn to be more Courageous?"

> **"[Each of us] is a hero-in-waiting who will be counted on to do the right thing when the time comes for [us] to make the heroic decision."**
>
> Philip Zimbardo[193]

We're all caught in a "vector of forces"[194] that make it hard to be consistently Authentic, Responsible and Courageous: social pressures, the diffusion of responsibility, being caught up in the present with a skewed view of the future, questions of personal identity, and so on.

Different people will see different threats in the same situation. Some people are more afraid of some threats than others. Some are more disposed to take risks than others – either because they're less anxious or require greater stimulation to get their adrenalin pumping – and a few are sufficiently risk-inclined for it to be considered a personality disorder.

Psychologist Professor Cynthia Pury found that 82% of people who'd committed Courageous acts used some kind of technique to enhance their bravery[195]. However, the questions of whether and how we can teach courage have been debated since the days of Plato and Aristotle. One of the most influential contributors is the 13th-century philosopher-priest Thomas Aquinas, who is widely considered the Catholic Church's greatest thinker. Aquinas wrote extensively on the topic and concluded that we cannot directly foster bravery (in ourselves or in others). Instead, he said, we need to work on two fronts: our good judgement and our sensitivity to fear. I think he was missing something, and the British Army agrees. Its approach to developing moral courage[196] talks of two developable components, both of which are equally applicable to physical, intellectual and aspirational courage:

1. 'Moral identity' – the Army works on developing soldiers' identity and judgement by working hard on its organisational culture. It aims to give team members clarity on the intent of an operation and autonomy in the way they achieve the objectives

2. 'Moral strength' – courage can be developed through two separate approaches: by reducing our sensitivity to fear, as Aquinas suggests, *and* by increasing our ability to feel that fear and do it anyway.

To help us understand how we put this into practice, I'm going to introduce you to my 'Resilience Bomb'.

Boston's Resilience Bomb™

A few years ago, my colleague Bernard Cooke and I came up with a model for coaching resilience. It worked and it looked good in PowerPoint, but it was

Boston's Resilience Bomb™

lacking something. It wasn't until 2011, when I was discussing stress in Madrid with people at Gucci Group, that my uninspiring flowchart evolved into the complex work of art you see here. The image summarises what happens when we encounter a fear-inducing stimulus and thus offers insights into how we can control our response.

Our uncontrolled response to fear works like this:

1. we encounter a 'stimulus' – a triggering event of some kind, whether it's a natural phenomenon, something someone else does, or some information (here it's the bomb)

2. perceive the stimulus as a threat (hence the eyes are in red)

3. we decide (hence the brain), that we lack the necessary resources to deal with that threat – after all, if we think we can handle it with ease, there's no need to be afraid

4. this belief triggers a physiological and emotional response: our *heart* pumps faster, we start sweating, our production of adrenalin and cortisol increases

5. finally, we react (the limbs): we freeze, lash out or run away – either literally or metaphorically – in a manner that is less productive than we might have liked.

Boosting our ability to take Courageous action means intervening at one or more of these stages. Wherever we intervene, we're attempting to shift the balance of control between two critical parts of the brain – echoing Robert Biswas-Diener's findings that 'feeling the fear' and 'doing it anyway' are two independent processes.

We're wired to make assumptions about threats almost instantaneously, using what Nobel Prize winner Daniel Kahneman[197] calls 'System 1' – the collection of mental processes that drives fast, intuitive, unconscious and emotional decision making. My clients and I find it more helpful to call it 'Amy' – short for the amygdala, one of the brain structures at the heart of System 1[198].

The other part of the brain, which Kahneman calls 'System 2', is more rational, data-driven and conscious.

Its decision-making processes are largely the domain of the pre-frontal cortex. As I've said, it's often nicknamed 'the CEO of the brain' but we'll call it 'the PFC' – using 'CEO' in this context can cause us to underestimate Amy's power over our thoughts, emotions and behaviour.

Amy's primed for fairly simple pleasure vs pain decisions, and she drives the instinctive response to a threatening stimulus outlined above. She also thinks and moves a great deal quicker than the PFC and would happily make all our decisions for us. If we're going to respond differently to the threats around us, we need to tackle Amy and give the PFC the time it needs to figure out a better response. This means taking one or more of four important actions.

1. Align heart, mind and body

To give the PFC a fighting chance, we need to quieten Amy by gaining control over our emotional and physiological reaction to the threat. We need to clear out the stress hormone cortisol that fogs up our minds and reduce the production of adrenalin, which is pressuring Amy for a fight or flight response.

Your baseline ability to align heart, mind and body is predominantly determined by two factors:

a. your personality traits that are determined through a combination of genetics and life experience

b. your chosen lifestyle – the decisions you make (often habitually rather than consciously) regarding what you eat, drink and do to keep your brain and body fit for purpose, and the level of stimulation you seek daily.

There's not a lot you can do about your personality but you can change your behaviours. Taking a longer-term, strategic approach to aligning heart, mind and body means making healthy, sustainable lifestyle choices. The armed forces recognised this a very long time ago. Enlightened corporations coach employees how to keep their bodies resilient to the stresses and strains of their work rather than treating their bodies as taxis that transport their brains from one place to another.

The tactical approach to aligning heart, mind and body is to use techniques to help us manage our emotions 'in the moment'. Most are rooted in meditation and hypnosis. Unfortunately, they are typically met with cynicism in a corporate environment. Now I consider myself very, very sceptical and it's with reservations that I originally tried these techniques myself. However, the corporate environment has come up with absolutely *nothing* that helps leaders and their people manage their emotions (and their physical effect) in challenging situations. Instead, we tend to respond to stress by eating sugary, fatty food, getting drunk, smoking, shopping, taking drugs and watching hours of television. Physiologically, none of these is helpful: while each promises a temporary release of some kind, in the longer term they increase our baseline anxiety *and* trigger the release of dopamine in the brain. Dopamine works by creating two parallel sensations: a craving for further reward and a fear that such rewards might not be forthcoming.

Thankfully, modern neuroscience has started to validate some of the techniques that actually *do* help us gain control of our fear. For instance, some of the Resilience Bomb tactics and strategies my colleagues and I use in our work have been shown to[199]:

a. trigger the release of serotonin, oxytocin and gamma-aminobutyric acid, which are associated with actual happiness rather than the mere promise of it

b. alter brain activity, including in the PFC

c. create lasting physical changes in the brain – which continues to develop late into our lives

d. boost our immune system – e.g. tripling our bodies' ability to mobilise flu antibodies[200].

Try this technique based on something Dr Peter Grünewald showed me when we were working together at one of the business schools a few years back[201]. You need to complete each step before reading the next. It'll take about five minutes.

Step 1:   Spend a minute writing about something that's bothering you – a real source of stress at the moment, which has yet to be resolved. Write freely; whatever comes into your head. The structure isn't important.

Step 2:   Slow down and deepen your breathing, tracking the air from your nostrils deep into those parts of your lungs that don't typically get enough fresh air due to the shallow way we breathe in our sedentary lives. Count slowly to five (in your head!) as you inhale, then slowly to five as you exhale. Don't hold your breath[202]. Breathing this way slows the heart and convinces the fear centres in the brain that everything is okay. It also focuses us on the present, preventing us from worrying about what might happen or has happened in the past.

Step 3:   Once you've read the instructions for this step, close your eyes and create a mental picture of something, someone or some event that makes you really happy. Take time to bring up the visual details – the colours, shapes, hairstyles, clothing, etc. Then introduce auditory detail – the sounds, voices, words and so on. Then locate the emotion. Literally find where you feel it in your body. When you've done that, open your eyes and proceed to step 4.

Step 4: Spend another minute writing about the same subject as before. Again, the structure is irrelevant. Write whatever comes into your head.

Step 5: Compare what you wrote in Step 1 with what you wrote in Step 4. What's different? The vast majority of people I've tried this with have noticed substantial differences. I'd tell you what they are, but then you might skip the exercise!

You'll notice that one of the steps involved visualisation. It's a technique athletes use very successfully to rehearse for major events. I hear there's empirical evidence that their motor neurones fire just as if they're actually doing the thing they're visualising. In 2012 Dutch and Chinese psychologists found that reminiscing about good times makes us feel physically warmer and increases our tolerance to cold and pain.[203] Similarly, many survivors of concentration camps coped with starvation by recalling delicious meals they'd eaten in the past. Our awareness of our physiological and emotional states seems to be processed by the same systems in the brain – most notably the anterior insular cortex. Thus, if we can change one state through visualisation (and breathing), we'll affect the other.

2. Reassess the threat

As philosophers, psychologists and self-help writers have been telling us for millennia[204], it's not people, things or events themselves that create emotional reactions in us, it's the way we think about those people, things or events.

The evidence suggests that courage is increased by taking time to reflect – time that allows us to *reassess the threat*. In a similar vein, the better people are at assessing risk across a range of situations, the more likely they are to take Courageous action[205].

So, how do we do it? First, grab yourself a blank sheet of paper. At the top, describe the situation in as few words as possible, including the Courageous action you're afraid to take – for example, "My boss is embezzling funds and I'm afraid to report him to the authorities." Then write your answers to the following questions:

- What is the worst that could happen if you take the Courageous course of action? (e.g. "People won't believe me, they'll think I'm disloyal, and my boss will take revenge on me.")

- What is the absolute best that could happen? Be imaginative here; it really does need to be the other extreme to your worst case scenario. (e.g. "He'll get what he deserves, I'll get promoted and people will hail me as a role model of integrity.")

- What other possible outcomes are there? ("He'll be reprimanded but will still be my boss", etc.)

- What are you assuming about the motives, character traits and capabilities of the people involved? ("I'm assuming my team will believe him over me", "I'm assuming he's the kind of person who can and will take revenge", etc.)

- How probable is each of these outcomes?

- How positive/negative is each of them, on a scale from +10 to -10?

- What hidden opportunities are there in this situation? ("I get to test my integrity in a really difficult situation", "We could change the culture of the team for the better", etc.)

3. Reassess your resources

Just as Amy makes some very quick, intuitive assumptions about the threat we're facing, she quickly and sometimes erroneously assesses the resources we have available to deal with that threat. The reality is, there is a whole range of them. Some are external (the people, materials and processes around us); others are internal. It's the latter I'll focus on here.

Internal resources fall into three categories: physical, emotional and intellectual. Most of us aren't great at predicting how we'll think, feel and act in the presence of a future threat. And when we are threatened, our ability to assess our capabilities is often compromised; just as we might overestimate the threat, so we can underestimate our ability to deal with the emotional ramifications of acting courageously.

> "Fear is that little darkroom where negatives are developed."
>
> Michael Pritchard, Green Day[206]

Tactics to use 'in the moment'

a. **Accept your limitations:** often it helps simply to accept that we don't know everything. Situations that challenge us as leaders might involve intricate politicking, variable and unclear levels of competence amongst our staff and fellow leaders, uncertainty as to whether the information we *do* have is correct and complete, and/or attention from external stakeholders. Similarly, we have to accept that we will be surprised: it's the 'unknown unknowns' that will get us[207]. The critical thing is to learn how we deal with surprises and work on improving our ability to do so.

b. **Name and reframe your assumptions:** as we discussed when we looked at *reassessing the threat*, name all the assumptions you are making about yourself in the situation – your physical, emotional and intellectual capacity to deal with the challenge. Then use the same six questions to challenge those assumptions.

c. **Turn dilemmas into inspiration:** if we're facing a dilemma, each of the prospective courses of action can be a source of inspiration for ways to improve the quality of action we take. We can draw on this inspiration before we begin to implement our chosen course of action.

QUESTION 7

Pick a challenge you've been thinking about as you've been reading this book. What resources do you have available to you that could help you take Courageous action in the face of that challenge? (*Some people find it helpful to answer this question by providing as many endings as possible to the sentence "I can do it because..."*)

Strategies to use in the longer term

Strategically, there are four things we can do to improve our perceptions of the internal resources available to us. The first is to seek high quality feedback from others. Importantly, we need to pay due attention to the positives – we're all far too adept at focusing on the negatives.

Another strategy is to properly prepare, which helps us marshal our internal *and* external resources in advance and gives us clarity as to our capabilities.

A third is to *practise* being Courageous – whether being Courageous means taking a moral stand, unlearning tightly held 'truths' or skiing down a black run. This kind of practice increases our confidence in our ability to deal with apparently threatening situations; it conditions our bodies to make us less susceptible to the physiological triggers that produce a fear response; it role models courage for those around us.

The armed forces make considerable use of both preparation and practice. They plan relentlessly, always knowing "no plan survives first contact with the enemy," and they subject their people to frequent tests of courage.

A fourth strategy is to change your identity. On the face of it, this sounds rather extreme. You might even say it's inAuthentic to change one's identity in order to cope with a particular situation. However, our responses to threatening situations are generally driven by our narrative about *who we are*. If I believe I'm a shy person, for instance, I'm more likely to feel threatened by the requirement to share a personal story with a roomful of strangers. If 'independent' is a core part of my identity, I'm less likely to ask for help; if I believe I'm empathetic, I might have greater faith in my capacity to deal with a situation that's challenging on a personal level.

The identities we create for ourselves can limit our potential and even make us miserable. We have the power to adjust them – we simply need will, and the right tools. It's not easy, but it is possible. Every one of us has faced fear of some kind and come out winning. We might not have won medals or Nobel prizes for it, but we *have* been Courageous. When we recognise that courage, rather than assuming courage is something other people have, the easier it is to own our ability to be Courageous – to make it a part of our identity. When we do that, the biases in Chapter 15 start to lose their power. When we're Authentic and accept that there are times and situations when we're brave and times and situations when we're not, we free ourselves up to be a little more Courageous in future.

In summary

In this chapter, we've used Boston's Resilience Bomb to identify and explore three ways of reducing the fear: aligning heart, mind and body; reassessing the threat; and reassessing the resources available (in and around us) that will help us deal with that threat. We've yet to look at the fourth step, 'do it anyway' – the step we take if our attempts to reduce the fear have failed. Arguably, it's at this point that courage *really* kicks in, and it's to this point that we turn our attention in the next chapter.

17

How to 'feel the fear and do it anyway'®†

● ● ●

> **"I have learnt by actual stress of imminent danger that self-control is more indispensable than gunpowder..."**
>
> Sir Henry Morton Stanley GCB,
> 19th-century explorer

"ALIGNING HEART, MIND

and body", "reassessing the threat" and "reassessing our resources" are all attempts by the PFC to convince Amy that everything's okay so we can do the Courageous thing. If none of those approaches works, we're left with three options.

The first is to promise Amy something so valuable and so certain that her desire for it will overwhelm her fear. Maybe a massage, then a sumptuous meal and a bottle of your favourite wine tonight if she'll let you fire that troublesome supplier this afternoon.

Or you could convince her that she's more scared of something else – the avoidance of which will produce Courageous action. This option is artfully used in the military, As Major Matt Cansdale at Sandhurst told me, "Even people who are 'in sweats' before a parachute jump wouldn't consider not jumping. We build such strong teams that people would rather die than be embarrassed in front of their friends." The British Army effectively convinces soldiers' amygdalae to pay greater attention to the

---

† Feel the Fear and Do It Anyway® is the registered trademark of The Jeffers/Shelmerdine Family Trust and is used with their permission.

social threat of embarrassment than the mortal threat of serious injury or death.

We can help the PFC shout louder – either by feeding it more fuel or by making it stronger

It's the same mechanism that once spurred a teenage boy to save a fellow student's life. He saw a man attacking a girl and ran to her aid. Only when he was halfway there did he realise her assailant was armed with a knife and was stabbing rather than punching her. This dramatically increased the mortal threat he was facing, prompting him to reconsider his actions. But now he had an audience and, by his own admission (over a beer or two), it was the fear of them thinking he was a coward that spurred him on.

A more sedate, office-based equivalent of this approach would be to address your fear of having a difficult conversation with your boss by promising five friends and five colleagues that you'll do it by the end of the week.

Our third option when we can't convince Amy everything's okay, and she's still shouting in the hope of getting her way is to help the PFC shout louder. It's certainly not an easy option. The PFC may be clever, but Amy is equipped with an impressive arsenal of influential weapons that has been sharpened and upgraded over countless generations.

Courage as a muscle

The battle between Amy and the PFC is a battle of wills. If we're going to increase the PFC's ability to win that battle, we need to increase our willpower[208]. The British Army's classic handbook *Serve to Lead* describes courage as "the fixed resolve not to quit; an act of renunciation which must be made not once but many times by the power of the will. Courage is willpower."[209]

One critical leap, which I've not seen elsewhere, is to link this description of courage as willpower to the latest research on willpower itself, led by

Professor Roy Baumeister at Florida State University. If, as the research suggests, self-control works like a muscle[210] then so, too, does courage. If that's the case, we suddenly find ourselves with a whole range of ways to develop courage in ourselves and others.

We strengthen our muscles by exercising them and feeding them fuel. It's the same with Courage: although the British Army didn't previously use these terms, the military training regime works on a principle of repeat-edly working the courage muscle, keeping it toned and making it stronger through exposure to activities that test it to its limits.

Turbo-Courage

Thinking of courage as a muscle offers another interesting insight. We store reserves in our muscles that allow us to manifest that extra boost of energy at the end of a race or when we're threatened with physical danger. It's the same with willpower – and, I've no doubt, with Courage.

Another factor that's critical to the development of courage is that willpower also appears to operate as a single muscle. There is a single mechanism (the PFC) that we use for a whole range of activities. When this single muscle is tired from exerting willpower over tasks like decision-making and resisting impulses to overindulge, it will be less able to exert willpower in other activities. Perhaps that's why some soldiers who demonstrate remarkable physical courage on the battlefield also commit adultery – with their single store of courage depleted it's much harder to manifest moral courage in the face of sexual temptation. It doesn't make their actions any more forgivable, but it does give us insight into the moral transgressions of others.

Our intellectual courage is also affected when our PFC is fatigued by exercising willpower in unrelated activities. For instance, when our willpower is depleted our scores in tests of IQ and logic drop[211] and we're more likely to choose small, quick wins over larger, guaranteed long-term ones[212].

Baumeister cites a wealth of evidence suggesting our aspirational courage is also affected by changes in self-control. For example: people who were coached in one of three interest areas (managing their personal finances, managing their studies, or getting fitter) also became better in the other two areas. Not only that but they smoked fewer cigarettes, drank less alcohol, procrastinated less *and* ate more healthily[213].

But now for some bad news. Baumeister recalls a survey of more than a million people around the world, in which respondents were asked about their strengths and weaknesses. The least cited character strength? Self-control. The number one failing? Self-control[214]. And the number one reason Americans gave for struggling to fulfil their goals, in a survey cited by another willpower guru, Kelly McGonigal[215]? Yep: self-control. And, as McGonigal points out, we also tend to *overestimate* our willpower. So, how can we overcome these sizeable obstacles to help us 'feel the fear and do it anyway'?

Strategies to build that muscle: PT for the PFC

a. **Create a new habit**[216]. It doesn't really matter what you choose, as long as it requires willpower and you repeat it again and again, ideally for a period of 90 days. Your chosen habit should also be something that has a point in itself, though, otherwise you'll give up. I started with flossing – yes, flossing! We all know it's good for us and it takes about 60 seconds, but for most of us it's not nearly as habitual as brushing our teeth, so it takes willpower to do it every single day.

b. **Meditate.** Meditation increases blood flow to the PFC, just as **exercise** increases the flow of blood to our muscles. It's also an act of self-control in its own right. Obviously, it takes willpower to build meditation into our busy lives but, if you can invest as much time each day as a smoker invests in a single cigarette break, you'll soon see improvements.

c. **Use physical exercise.** Taking regular exercise requires us to flex our self-control, which strengthens it. It also increases our heart rate variability, itself a powerful predictor of willpower[217], and increases our body's ability to cope with Amy's stress response[218].

Tactics: muscles need fuel

There are two types of fuel: physical and psychological.

Physical fuels: food, drink and sleep

Since 2007, a number of studies, including Baumeister's, have suggested blood-sugar levels play a significant role in the PFC's ability to solve problems, make decisions and keep Amy under control[219]. Baumeister frequently cites research led by Professor Shai Danziger[220] at Tel Aviv University, which found that judges' intake of food and drink dramatically affected their likelihood of awarding parole. As an individual offender, your chances of being awarded freedom were 65% if you were seen straight after a break – during which the judges would eat and drink, restoring their glucose levels. If you happened to come in just *before* the break, your chances of getting parole would be between zero and 12%. These findings, that no facts about you or your case had nearly as much impact on your fate as a cup of tea and a biscuit, held over a total of 1,112 rulings.

Baumeister's research suggests glucose acts as fuel for the PFC, helping it shout louder than Amy. More recent research[221] leads me to suspect glucose plays a more complex role. To me, it seems more likely that glucose, or even just the promise of glucose, either distracts Amy with something she likes, reassures the PFC that fuel is on its way, or both.

Either way, the evidence suggests our willpower, and hence our courage, is best served by eating throughout the day, opting for slow-release foods with a low glycaemic index – like vegetables, nuts, *some* raw fruits, cheese, fish, meat, olive oil and other 'good' fats. White bread, potatoes, white rice, snacks and fast food produce spikes in our sugar levels and with them peaks and troughs in our PFC's ability to overrule Amy.

Sleep also makes a huge difference. Go 24 hours without sleep, or sleep four or five hours a night for a week and you'll be as impaired as if you had a blood alcohol level of 0.1%. Go ten days on four hours a night and you'll be operating as if you've gone 48 hours with no sleep at all[222] – the equivalent of being over the legal limit for driving in most countries in the world. Is it any wonder that the wired corporate executive and occasional politician make decisions they later come to regret?

While most people across 18 countries believe they sleep for approximately eight hours each night[223], research suggests we overestimate the amount of sleep we get by almost 90 minutes[224].

If you want to make the most of the sleep you do get, you'd be wise to try meditating and/or avoiding work, emails, food, caffeine, alcohol and food in the two hours before you go to bed. Succumbing to any of those temptations reduces your percentage of deep sleep – the type of sleep our body needs to repair itself.

Dutch Courage

Many native English speakers use the term "Dutch Courage" to refer to the fact that alcohol appears to make us more Courageous. Apparently it's a reference to soldiers drinking Dutch gin before battle.

How can alcohol increase courage if it reduces willpower? It's an inhibitor, reducing some of the physiological symptoms of a stress response and impairing the PFC, causing us to underestimate the risks and overestimate both the upsides and our own abilities. Thus, alcohol works by reducing the fear rather than increasing our ability to 'do it anyway' – and in many cases it leaves us at Amy's mercy, rather than aiding the PFC.

Psychological fuels: authenticity and responsibility

We can help the PFC in its battle with Amy by connecting it with a higher purpose, whether that's by tapping into authenticity, responsibility or both. The best ways to use authenticity to fuel courage are to develop our Authentic Insight and hone an Authentic Intent. Where Insight is concerned, try focusing on the following:

- *Ask yourself: "Have I run out of courage or am I just saving energy?"* As with our other muscles, we tend to hold some courage in reserve.

- *Ask yourself: "Am I strengthening or weakening my long-term Courage?"* Authentic Insight enables us to recognise that, every time we fail to be Courageous, we make it harder for next time. We should show courage and strengthen that willpower muscle.

- *Take responsibility for your failures, then forgive yourself* and challenge yourself to do better.

- *Draw strength from courageous acts you've performed in the past*, without triggering a 'licence to sin' (as in "I was Courageous yesterday, so I've earned the right to take all the easy options today").

- *Know your kryptonite.* Knowing what tempts us to be less-than-Courageous, and in which circumstances our willpower will be depleted, helps us prepare against future temptations.

- *Recognise that the future 'you' is still you.* Accepting this helps us recognise that we won't feel less pressured or fearful next time around.

Honing our Authentic Intent gives us clarity of purpose, which can help us resist temptations to take a less-than-Courageous course of action. To help us do so, Bill George[225] recommends we identify our values, principles and boundaries as leaders.

QUESTION 8
Your values, principles and boundaries...

a. **What are your core values?** *(You may have already used the 'Values exercise' in Appendix 1 to help you with this, or you may be clear enough already.)*

....

....

....

....

....

....

b. **Based on these values, what are your leadership principles?**
(Start by filling a page with as many sentences as possible that start with the words "In my role as a leader, I will always..." Then decide which 3-5 of those sentences you would teach to others.)

....

....

....

....

....

....

   c. **What are your ethical boundaries?** *(3-5 sentences that start with the words "In my role as a leader, I will never…" Again, it's best to generate many statements, then choose the 3-5 that you would teach to others.)*

      ....

      ....

      ....

      ....

      ....

   d. **For each of the commitments in (b) and (c), how will you respond if you're being tempted to break that commitment?** *(Deciding in advance what we will do in specific situations reduces the mental energy required when the event occurs.)*

      ....

      ....

      ....

      ....

      ....

One of the most compelling ways to use your answers to these questions is to hand them to the one person you trust most to challenge you – someone who isn't subordinate to you – then check in regularly on how well you've stuck to your commitment.

    Another option is to put the sentences on two cards next to the bathroom mirror at home ("I will…" and "I won't…"). Looking ourselves in the mirror and seeing those commitments each night before we go to bed can have a powerful effect.

Authenticity is fuel from *within*. Responsibility is a powerful fuel that has its source *outside* of us. Any of the Three Domains of Responsibility can help.

Will King, founder of King of Shaves, drew courage from the Personal domain: friends and family had invested in his business and he knew if he didn't make a success of it he'd be letting them down.

When Anne Mulcahy became CEO of Xerox in 2001, it was Professional responsibility that fuelled her courage. The organisation was close to bankruptcy and its financial practices were being investigated. She talks of "waking up in the middle of the night and thinking about 96,000 employees and retirees and what would happen if things went south."[226] The sense of responsibility she felt towards her staff (and the support it brought her) was what galvanised her, enabling her to push back on outsiders' insistence that Xerox file for bankruptcy and save the company. Seven years later she was named 'CEO of the Year'[227].

When students in a study of willpower were told that doing their best would help researchers discover a cure for Alzheimer's, they demonstrated higher levels of self-control than those with no such motivation[228]. It's the same mechanism (Societal responsibility) that helped Nelson Mandela maintain his levels of moral and physical courage for 18 years on Robben Island.

So how do we *actually* draw on our sense of responsibility to boost our courage in the moment? I'll offer three suggestions, some of which you may already be using:

- **Take time to connect with your 'higher purpose'.** Visualise it, or simply spend some time thinking about the people, thing or cause for which you feel Responsible.

- **Tie yourself in.** Make a commitment and make it public. The people around us – at work and outside of it – are all potential sources of support and nourishment that can boost our reserves when we're running low. One powerful option is to create what Bill George calls

'True North groups' – our own personal boards of directors, whom we meet regularly and who act as highly trusted personal and professional advisors.

- **Get infected.** Willpower and courage are contagious. We 'catch' courage from people we consider to be sufficiently like (or connected to) us. You can capitalise on this by finding some Courageous role models and spending more time with them.

QUESTION 9

To put this into practice, revisit one of the challenges you've been considering while reading this book, and ask yourself what 'psychological fuel' you can draw upon to help you meet that challenge.

In summary

Courage works like a muscle – a single muscle that powers all four types of Courageous action. If we want to increase our ability to 'feel the fear and do it anyway', we need to strengthen and feed that muscle. Building its strength means investing time and effort in the longer term. In the short term, we can give our courage a boost by managing our levels of physical energy and drawing on the psychological fuel of authenticity and responsibility.

• • •

Questions and commitments

•●•

Thinking further

I BELIEVE QUESTIONS are the true route to a deeper understanding and are more powerful than vast amounts of information. Even so, I've thrown a lot of information at you on the subject of courage. I've asked you to do some reflection along the way, exploring your own courage. You may or may not have done so, but I strongly encourage you to consider and discuss the following:

You

● In each of the spheres of my life, to what extent do others experience me as Courageous?

● What do I role-model to my team, colleagues and family?

You and your team (or family)

You can either answer these questions yourself, or use them as discussion points for a team meeting.

● To what extent are we as a team (or family) taking the Courageous path in the decisions we make at both an individual and unit level?

● To what extent do we challenge ourselves and our current ways of thinking?

- Choose three people who are close to you at home or work. Looking at each one individually, what forces make it hard for them to be Courageous? Then ask yourself:

  - What am I doing to contribute to this?

  - What threats (or supposed threats) in their relationships with others or the type of work they do makes it hard from them to be Courageous?

  - What assumptions are they making about their resources (within them and around them) that make it hard for them to be Courageous?

Your organisation

- What are we doing as an organisation that our staff can see is Courageous?

- How Courageous do we seem to our external stakeholders? If we don't already know, how might we find out? What answers might we expect and what would we do with the information?

Your commitments

- Make one big commitment to yourself (in relation to being Courageous) and write it down.

....

....

....

....

....

• Clarify your commitment:

   a. Who else is it important to?

....

....

   b. Why is it important, to you and to them?

....

....

• Go back to those three significant people in your life (at work or otherwise) and make this commitment explicitly to them. (As I said in Chapter 7, you could wait until you've finished the book before you do this, but I strongly suggest you share your commitment before reading on.)

•●•

PART
5

Authentic +
Responsible +
Courageous

A quick recap

• ● •

I FIND THE FOLLOWING questions act as a helpful summary of the three ARC qualities:

Authentic	"To what extent am I being true to myself, genuine in my interactions and acting in accordance with my beliefs?"
Responsible	"To what extent does my appreciation and prioritisation of my responsibilities optimise my contribution to the sustained success of the people and things around me?"
Courageous	"What does this situation demand of me that I'm afraid to step up to?"

We've gone deeper than this, though, throughout the book, so let's take a few minutes to look back on what we've covered.

What it means to be Authentic, Responsible and Courageous

In Part Two, we identified Four Spheres of Authenticity:

AUTHENTIC ACTION

Acting in accordance with
our Authentic Intent, rather
than reacting to external
threats, inducements, social
expectations or rewards.
Demonstrating a visible
connection between what
we believe, what we say and
what we do.

AUTHENTIC INTERACTION

Being genuine, present
and transparent in our
relationships with others,
rather than presenting a façade.
Communicating in ways that
make it clear what we stand for.
Being honest about our opinions,
flaws, mistakes and contributions
(good and bad).

AUTHENTIC INTENT

Approaching life and leadership with a sense of purpose that is
drawn from our core values and beliefs. In the short term, this means
honestly appraising our intentions for a given situation.
In the long term, it involves us aspiring to be the best version
of ourselves that we can possibly be.

AUTHENTIC INSIGHT

An honest, non-judgemental appraisal of our own strengths and
weaknesses. Recognising and understanding our habits, motivations,
emotions and perspectives, including understanding their origins and
their effects on our behaviour. Appreciating the fact that some of our
deeply held attitudes, beliefs and assumptions contradict each other.
Taking ownership for the way we respond to situations.

In Part Three, we saw that being Responsible requires us to progress
through three stages. We need to…

1. Realise what it is we're Responsible for, which can include people
   (living, dead and yet to come), institutions and abstract entities like
   culture, process and organisational history

2. Prioritise amongst competing responsibilities

3. Act on that prioritisation.

In order to fully Realise the extent of our responsibilities in an increasingly interdependent world, it can be helpful to consider Three Domains of Responsibility:

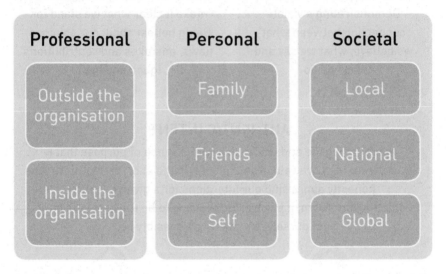

In Part Four, I offered Three Dimensional Courage to help broaden our appreciation of what it means to be Courageous, and deepen our understanding of the fears that get in the way:

ACTION	Mortal	Social	Psychological
Physical			
Moral			
Intellectual			
Aspirational			

We explored the three types of threat and four types of Courageous action, suggesting that:

- **Physical courage** comes from the body and is driven by a desire to defeat the opposition, which includes other people, illness and the forces of nature

- **Moral courage** has its source in our sense of right and wrong, is driven by our desire to do what is morally right and resides in the heart

- **Intellectual courage** is cognitive, residing in the mind, and is driven by our desire to do what is logically right

- **Aspirational courage** springs from our sense of our own and others' potential and could be conceived as residing in the spirit; the motivation here is to be the best we can be.

Why we sometimes struggle

Habits, roles and fears sometimes make it hard to be truly Authentic. I told you about the six most common fears in my research, which seem to boil down to a fear of being rejected or persecuted.

We looked at why we sometimes fail to Realise, Prioritise and Act on our responsibilities. We saw that failures to Realise are often due to a lack of systemic thinking, and that failing to Act typically suggested either we lacked the courage to turn prioritisation into action or our prioritisation hadn't been truly Authentic. I also shared the most common reasons for being less-than-Responsible when prioritising:

1. I can't do it, because I don't have sufficient time, resources or band-width, or I lack the skills, intellect or ability

2. I shouldn't do it, because it's none of my business, or I'm afraid of what it might cost me

3. Someone else will do it and/or there's no reason I should make the first move

4. I don't want to do it, because I don't have the energy, the potential recipient doesn't deserve it, or it's just not 'me' to do so

5. I can't decide right now because I don't have enough information, or the situation is too complicated.

We considered six obstacles to being Courageous, other than the fear itself:

1. Fear is a fundamental instinct that keeps us alive

2. The way each of us was brought up increases our sensitivity to particular threats and affects our attitude

3. Humans are naturally predisposed to cognitive biases that work against Courageous action

4. The lack of courage we see around us is contagious.

5. The pressure to be Responsible can hold us back

6. Authentic Insight can affect our perception of the threat and the resources we have to deal with it.

Why ARC is worth the effort

In Part One, we looked at the demand for Authentic, Responsible, Courageous leadership in a world that is increasingly complex and interconnected, and where trust is in decline. We heard how the three ARC qualities help us manifest many of the other qualities people look for in their leaders. I shared a number of benefits I've seen for teams, organisations and their stakeholders when leaders are more Authentic, Responsible and Courageous – including ARC's impact on performance, staff and stakeholder buy-in, the clarity of a team or organisation's direction and its capacity to continually deliver.

We also recognised that there's a selfish streak in all of us, but that there are numerous benefits to individual leaders who are Authentic, Responsible and Courageous. This style of leadership is rewarding and sustaining morally and materially; it's more energising; it earns us respect and connects us with the people and world around us; it helps us get what we want; it drives learning, performance and career progression.

How we can get better at ARC

We have explored at a number of ways to overcome the various obstacles in order to be more Authentic, Responsible and Courageous. We walked six routes to authenticity and six steps to being sustainably Responsible. We used the Resilience Bomb to reduce fear and developed our courage muscles to help us 'feel the fear and do it anyway'. Some of these approaches drew on the fact that the three ARC qualities sometimes aid each other, and sometimes get in each other's way. It's to this 'dance' that we'll turn next. But first, take a few minutes to think about how these three qualities have interacted for you in the past 24 hours.

ARC in the past 24 hours

QUESTION 1

Try looking at the past 24 hours and write down the ways in which you've been Authentic, Responsible and Courageous.

....

....

....

....

....

....

....

....

QUESTION 2

Now write down the ways in which you could have been more Authentic, Responsible and Courageous.

....

....

....

....

....

....

....

QUESTION 3

Look at the two lists above and consider the ways each of the three ARC qualities interacted. How did your authenticity, responsibility and courage help each other in your answers to Question 1? How did they hinder each other in Question 2?

....

....

....

....

....

● ● ●

20

Bringing the three strands together

• ● •

AT BP, IN 2005 AND 2010, it was arguably a lack of Responsible, Courageous leadership that contributed to two disasters. Prior to the explosion at the company's Texas City refinery on 3 March 2005, staff had repeatedly questioned the CEO's demands for 25% cuts across all parts of the business. Somewhere in middle management, key people failed to be courageously Responsible for the safety of Texas City staff and residents.

Elsewhere in the organisation, though, its leaders and staff were being highly Responsible. They'd recently finished developing a unique, low odour fuel called Opal aimed at reducing petrol sniffing by indigenous Australians – which it did, by up to 94%[229].

Understandably, in the wake of the Texas refinery disaster, Responsibility gained new prominence, becoming one of four key values: "progressive, responsible, innovative, and performance driven"[230]. Nevertheless, the same culture of prioritising profitability over safety appears to have contributed to the Gulf of Mexico's Deepwater Horizon disaster five years later. It wasn't all BP's fault, of course: its partners Transocean and Halliburton have been criticised for their contributions, as have the policies and practices of the governments accused of insufficiently regulating the oil industry[231] – any or all of whom could have been more Responsible and more Courageous.

Importantly, though, BP has since updated its company values again

– this time to include 'courage'. There's a new emphasis on "speaking up", "standing by what we believe" and "striving to do the right thing" as well as the intellectual courage that was evident in previous recent iterations of the company's values. There's an element of authenticity in the new values, too – in phrases like "unafraid to ask for help" and "honest with ourselves".

Weaving all three ARC qualities into its company values is a good start, but we've seen how hard it is to be consistently Authentic, Responsible and Courageous – and to balance all three. Only time will tell whether BP can effect the culture change required to enable more than 85,000 people rise to that difficult challenge.

In watching BP, I'm reminded of a noble and challenging task one of the founding fathers of the United States of America, Benjamin Franklin, set himself back in the 18th century. He had identified thirteen virtues and decided to put a great deal of effort into living up to them. The problem was, whenever he was focused on one it seemed to come into conflict with one or more of the others: Order clashed with Industry, for example, when his task-focused, structured days were interrupted by clients wanting him to prioritise their needs over the things he'd already planned to get done.

Nevertheless, when Franklin later spoke of his attempts to follow that thirteen-week plan, he said "...on the whole, tho' I never arrived at the perfection I had been so ambitious of obtaining, but fell far short of it, yet I was, by the endeavour, a better and a happier man than I otherwise should have been if I had not attempted it."[232]

Like Franklin's and like BP's, our lives are complex systems. *We* are complex systems. To be truly effective, we need to know ourselves authentically, responsibly and courageously, to accept our complexities and imperfections while aspiring to be better. Judging ourselves too harshly makes us more anxious, less decisive, less productive and affects our physical and mental health[233]. Sure, it would be easier if we could describe ourselves in a single sentence. Personality profiling tools like Belbin, Myers-Briggs, FIRO-B and Hogan's 'Dark Side' all have a role to play in that – a role that many users forget is to *explore* that complexity, rather than replace it. But if we hide from our complexity we risk making ourselves less interesting and we make it easier for others to outmanoeuvre us. We reduce our ability to empathise and make it harder to manage the dance between authenticity, responsibility and courage.

As I said in Chapter 10, in the dance between the ARC qualities, we are generally prone to four mistakes, or 'miss-steps':

1. We remain static between two points – for example, rigidly fixed between being Authentic and being Responsible, unable to decide which to prioritise

2. We can embrace one and not the other(s) – as jeweller Gerald Ratner did in his scathingly irResponsible but highly Authentic description of his company's products; or as the boards of Enron and the Royal Bank of Scotland did when they responsibly but inauthentically insisted their organisations were at no risk of collapsing

3. We can confuse one with the other(s) – as I did, mistaking authenticity for courage when I was hailed as a hero for my actions during an armed robbery

4. We can try to compromise between them, which makes less of both.

The dance is not a compromise. It is not a 'cop out'. As Joseph Badaracco says in his book, *Leading Quietly*[234]: "Seeing the world as a complicated and uncertain place can serve as an excuse for not thinking about serious problems."

In my opinion, though, Badaracco sends mixed messages and asks leaders to expect less of themselves than they should. Sure, he's right that middle managers shouldn't confuse their day-to-day ethical conundrums with the epic struggles of the world, but the lives of each leader and the people they lead are epics in themselves.

Critically, among Badaracco's useful tips that help us "nudge, test, and escalate gradually"[235] he quotes E. Hamilton Lee's adage "There are old pilots and bold pilots, but no old, bold pilots". But E. Hamilton Lee was himself an old, bold pilot. He lived until the age of 103 and demonstrated enormous amounts of courage during his 27,812 hours flying planes, during which he covered 4.4 million miles (over 7 million kilometres). The man even spent his hundredth birthday co-piloting a plane from Ontario to the outskirts of Los Angeles[236].

The world *needs* its leaders to be more demanding of themselves where these three ARC qualities are concerned. Yes, it requires a dance, but the dance is about "keeping questions and purposes alive"[237], keeping things sufficiently fluid and honing our ability to notice and deal with changes in our environment. At its heart is the capacity to deal with paradox. The very concept of trust in leadership breeds a paradox – on one hand, people's trust in their leader is partly defined by that leader's consistency over time; on the other, leaders are having to adapt increasingly quickly to changes in their operating environment, and to changes of direction above and below.

The dance is largely about learning from those paradoxes, which means "not knowing or judging, but accepting that both sides and neither are true. It means looking at the relationship between the opposites and leaving all options open while exploring the wider context, until we arrive at a higher level of understanding and a new, more resolvable question emerges."[238]

Dancing well requires us to combine the three qualities, to conjoin them to make something better rather than diluting them with each other to make something worse. I find it helpful to combine the words themselves: to ask myself questions like "What would be the courageously Responsible course of action here?" or "How can I be courageously and responsibly Authentic in this meeting?"

Another approach is to picture the three qualities in a triangle, one on each point. The answer to many of the challenges we face in one corner of the triangle can come from looking at the mid-point between the other two. If I'm feeling smothered by my responsibilities, for instance, I could step out of that corner of the triangle and move to the mid-point between 'Authentic' and 'Courageous'.

I'm going to ask you to try this for yourself, but first I'd like to share some examples of other people dancing with the three ARC qualities.

ARC in use

Aligning directors and senior managers in a professional services firm

When we first met, "Bill" was a Partner at one of the world's largest professional services firms. One evening – over a meal of dim sum and red wine, which is probably a culinary crime – we discussed the team he was leading at the time. He'd managed to create a tight cadre of Partners, which is quite an achievement given that the structure of professional services firms typically encourages Partners to operate independently. Each grows his or her part of the business and is rewarded accordingly, which tends to breed more competition than collaboration.

Bill's Partner team had a clear vision that each member believed in; the team took on joint accountability for success and was making some bold decisions to turn the vision into a reality. What he couldn't work out was how to get the two levels of management below the Partners to adopt a similar attitude. Generally speaking, they were much more reactive and focused on their own projects, silos and/or career progression than on the overall vision for Bill's part of the firm.

I suggested that the Partners were united by the three ARC qualities: they had a vision that was Authentic to them. As a result, they felt genuinely

Responsible for its success. They'd been Courageous in generating the vision in the first place and their sense of Authentic responsibility for the shared endeavour fuelled them to make Courageous, entrepreneurial decisions in pursuit of their vision.

The directors and senior managers, on the other hand, were less authentically connected with the vision. It wasn't theirs; it was their bosses' baby. Consequently, they felt much less Responsible for it. Without authenticity and responsibility fuelling their Courage, few of the managers would take any risks for the good of the Partners' vision. The question, then, became how to connect these middle managers authentically with a shared endeavour, something for which they would all feel genuinely Responsible.

We wondered aloud if the answer was rooted in the reasons these managers felt compelled to compete: if ten managers are seeking promotion and there's only enough income to support three promotions, there's little incentive for one manager to help his peers to succeed. It's a situation that drives individualism, but it's not that different from the situation the Partners had started with: each Partner is rewarded for his or her contribution to the overall profits of the firm. Bill's team of Partners had overcome this divisive mechanism by focusing on collaborating to grow the pie. What if their middle managers could do the same? What if they had a single shared endeavour: to grow Bill's part of the firm to a size that could afford to promote all ten middle managers into more senior roles?

This is precisely the challenge Bill then took to them. He made it clear that he was looking for them to take on the leadership role in that part of the Firm – to replace him and the other Partners within the next three to five years.

"I've told them I want them to be driving our future growth because they are the future of this part of the business, not me," he said when we spoke a few weeks later. "I'm convinced that many of them have the ability and drive it takes, however, my main concern is that only one or two have the ARC qualities required to take on the leadership position."

What's needed most, Bill believes, is courage. He believes they'll increasingly feel more authentically connected to the vision, which will inspire them to take on responsibility. Then, he hopes, the combination of being Authentic and being Responsible will spur them to be more Courageous and thus fully occupy their roles as the future leaders of the business.

Authentic, Courageous responsibility drives a truly global career

For years, Britta had a sense that she was not quite living up to her potential. She had a higher calling burning away inside her that she hadn't truly accessed. She'd done a lot of good in the course of her work and she'd come a long way in her career. She's an Australian who relocated to London aged 26, where she worked her way up through one of the UK's most respected consultancies. In 2009, she joined Shell and since then she'd been travelling the world sharing her expertise with the company's leaders. But it was becoming increasingly clear that something was missing, that in order to be truly Authentic she needed to try something different.

So where did she look? Right between responsibility and courage. She looked about as far beyond herself as she could to find something to take responsibility for – something that would demand an awful lot of courage: negotiating a three-month sabbatical to enable her to take on a placement in a remote village in the northeast Indian state of Jharkhand. Her role: to coordinate the creation of much-needed infrastructure, and her support was two fellow Australians half a world away and intermittently available via phone and email. Her first job was to get a fence built to keep the elephants out – and that was the easy bit. Her work there was challenging on a number of levels, but highly rewarding. She made such a success of it that when she returned to Australia and got a new job in consultancy, her new employer agreed that she could take extra holiday to continue her work in India. Not only that, but the charity took her on as a non-executive member of its board.

Dancing into a career change

Jane had reached the top of her profession in PR and Communications. She'd been on the exec board of a couple of consultancies and one step from the board of a well-known pharmaceuticals company. All along, though, she'd felt it wasn't the right career for her. She talked of other paths she might have taken, other interests she might have pursued. She'd tried leaving it all behind, living on the other side of the world, but wherever she went she found herself falling back into the same old career. In ARC terms, two forces were pulling her back:

- she lacked the Authentic Insight to know what it was she *really* wanted to do

- having grown used to an impressive income, she felt Responsible for continuing to contribute financially to her family.

Finding the courage to change careers required her to resolve these two issues. Once she'd resolved the first and set her mind on becoming an executive coach, it took courage to resolve the conflict between her Authentic aspirations and her sense of responsibility to her family. Like Britta's, Jane's Authentic Intent came from reaching beyond herself. She realised that the thing she'd enjoyed most in her career to date was the responsibility she'd had for others – and, most importantly, for their development. Now, many aspiring coaches would have set up shop overnight and perhaps signed up for a six-week course in coaching. Jane's approach was at once Authentic, Responsible and Courageous: she found the best course she could, a challenging three year MSc programme at one of the world's leading business schools – quite a stretch for someone who left University twenty years before and doesn't consider herself particularly academic. Once there, she continued to act authentically, responsibly and courageously. She sought feedback and examined her own practice relentlessly; she learned, unlearned and re-learned at a pace that enabled her to evolve far faster than many of her peers; she sought additional training, travelling to the USA in search of the world's best trainers on one particular topic, and created learning groups to accelerate her own learning and theirs; she contributed to the wider coaching community through her involvement in one of the industry's biggest professional bodies. It's no wonder that, of everyone in her year group, Jane was the only student to be offered a role on the coaching faculty within weeks of finishing her final research project – or that she graduated with a distinction and a prize for outstanding achievement.

Jane and Britta are individuals, taking their own paths. They're both leaders: Britta has led in her role at Shell, in Jarkhand and in her consultancy role in Australia. Jane led in her previous career and acted less explicitly as an unofficial leader during the course of her MSc. Unless you're questioning your own choice of career or contribution to the world, their stories may be quite different to yours. So I'd like to offer another that might be closer to your *own* experience as a leader.

'The mighty three' drive decision making in a children's charity

Nicola is Director of the children's charity Wallace and Gromit's Grand Appeal – Wallace and Gromit being two characters created by Academy Award-winning Aardman Animations, whose directors are the charity's patrons. Since 1995, The Grand Appeal has raised £21 million for facilities, pioneering equipment and family accommodation for sick and critically ill babies and children across the south west of England and south Wales.

Nicola encountered the three ARC qualities through Jane, who has been coaching Nicola and her team since 2011. The words Authentic, Responsible and Courageous resonated with Nicola, so they used them as a means of working through some of the decisions she was facing at the time. Six months later, when I spoke to Nicola to find out more, she described the three ARC qualities as an "unbelievably accurate" appraisal of the core challenges facing her in her leadership. She has the three words on her office wall and refers to them as "the mighty triumvirate". "Authenticity is the absolute heart and core of The Grand Appeal," she said. "If people are going to invest in what we're trying to achieve, they need to trust us, believe that we're the right organisation to work with, that we're transparent and will do what we say we're going to do. They also need to know we're Responsible. It's incumbent on us to safeguard our donors' wishes and their money, and to respect the way they want to interact with the charity."

Rather modestly, Nicola suggested authenticity and responsibility are almost a given in the charity sector. The challenge for Nicola, when she first met Jane, was being truly Courageous. "The aspirations were there, but not the courage to make them reality," she said. "The charity sector isn't a brave world. The financial climate is tough, the sector is shrinking and we're not one of the huge 'super-charities' with a strong, diverse support base. But if you're not Courageous you stand still; you become lost in a mire of greyness. The coaching gave me permission to be Courageous."

Much of this permission came from Nicola's sense of what it means to be Authentic and Responsible. She recognised that she was favouring one responsibility over another: protecting herself and her team from the risks of doing something bigger, rather than being truly Responsible to The Grand Appeal's brand – 'to be brave and fun'. To resolve this tension, she used authenticity and responsibility as psychological fuel for courage – just as we saw in Chapter 17. She drew on her belief in what was right and her sense of duty to her team, her stakeholders and their shared endeavour – to help save and improve the lives of sick and critically ill babies and children. Since then, she says, the "mighty three" ARC qualities have always informed the decisions and actions she and her team have taken. Their milestone project in 2013, 'Gromit Unleashed', was a prime example. It's no easy task, populating one of the UK's largest cities with seventy giant fibreglass models of an animated dog, each decorated by a different artist and each to be auctioned off at the end of the summer. Turning the concept into reality required Nicola and her team to negotiate with twenty key stakeholders, only three of whom initially bought into the idea.

The auction raised more than £2.3 million and the trail of giant 'Gromits' sparked a plethora of associated fund-raising events. Indeed, Gromit Unleashed brought such a buzz to the city that summer that it won 'Tourist Event of the Year'.

"If we hadn't demonstrated authenticity, responsibility and courage, people wouldn't have trusted us enough to take the leap of faith that's needed to do something like this," she said. "If we'd been irresponsibly Courageous and taken on a project that was far beyond our reach, we'd have lost the goodwill of the community that supports us."

Your turn

Take any situation, decision or dilemma that you're struggling with right now. The chances are, the root of the problem is one of the three qualities. Work out which one, then put your finger on it – yes, I do mean on the page or screen in front of you. Now look at the centre-point on the line that runs between the other two qualities. Then ask yourself how the combination of those two qualities can guide you towards a robust, actionable decision. It's a strange concept at first, but it works. Asking yourself the following questions might help.

If your finger is resting on...	Ask yourself these two questions, one at a time...
Authentic	1. What needs (of my own and my stakeholders) should I consider in order to resolve this situation?
	2. How would the 'truest, bravest, smartest, most Responsible version of me' address the shared and apparently conflicting needs we all have?
Responsible	1. What would it look like if I realigned my responsibilities in a way that reflected my values in the healthiest, most sustainable way for myself and everyone involved?
	2. What do I need to grasp or let go of in order to move things forward?
Courageous	1. Who and what will suffer if I fail to act courageously in this situation?
	2. What do my core values demand of me?

In summary

Being Authentic, Responsible and Courageous requires us to maintain the dance, conjoining the three rather than compromising or diluting any of them. We work out which of the three ARC qualities is at the heart of our leadership challenge, then we look to the other two qualities for insight and inspiration. Sometimes inspiration comes in the form of information or answers; sometimes it comes in the form of better questions.

● ● ●

21

Where to from here?

•●•

THIS BOOK IS FULL of stories and if you've written in it yourself, it'll track your story, too: the challenges you face and the resources you have to help you be more Authentic, Responsible and Courageous.

Whether or not you've answered all the questions I've posed in this book, I'll be stunned if you've come this far without doing some good work. I imagine you'll also be left with some questions of your own. Some of those will be questions for you to answer, and some will be questions for the people around you. You might have some questions for me, too. If you do, I'd love to hear them – whether it's via the website or the 'ARC: Authentic + Responsible + Courageous' group on LinkedIn.

In this final chapter, I'd like to focus on what you do next. I'll revisit this book's original intent, then talk about the notion of 'mastering' the three ARC qualities and offer some practical tips for taking things forward. We'll end with a view of the future, where I'll ask you to imagine a world led by people who are truly Authentic, Responsible and Courageous.

The intent of this book was never to turn you into some legendary leader with a guaranteed place in the history books. None of the people and organisations we've held up as examples of authenticity, responsibility and courage in action are perfect. Few of those whose failures we've reviewed are outright villains. All of us have times when we're exemplifying these three ARC qualities and times when we're failing to do so. Our working lives are a blend of big and small decisions, personal challenges and professional tensions.

My intention with this book was to offer you something I've found incredibly useful, to celebrate the ways in which you're already Authentic, Responsible and Courageous, to walk with you as you've grappled with how hard it can be, to offer suggestions, and to encourage you to keep at it – to keep raising your standards and those of others.

That's why I want to end the book by talking about 'mastering' the three ARC qualities.

Mastering ARC by mastering the dance

In his book, *Drive*[239], Daniel Pink observes that mastery in any domain abides by three specific principles:

1. Mastery is a mindset

2. Mastery is pain

3. Mastery is an asymptote

The chances are the word 'asymptote' currently means nothing to you. Don't worry: I'll cover each of the three rules in turn.

1. Mastery is a mindset

The pursuit of mastery requires us to see our abilities not as finite, but as infinitely improvable. It requires us to gain our primary satisfaction not from the things we achieve, but from the things we learn, and to welcome effort as a means of getting better at something that matters.

In Chapter 20, we saw how thinking of the three qualities as a triangle can help us resolve some of the challenges we face in trying to live up to these qualities. Mastery requires us to add another dimension to that triangle – a vertical dimension that turns our ARC triangle into a three-sided pyramid (or 'tetrahedron' if you prefer that term). Each

of the corners of its base represents one of the three ARC qualities. Each of the lines extending upwards shows us getting better at each of those qualities. As we master the three, we move upwards. As we move upwards, the three qualities come closer together, more integrated with each other.

In adopting this mindset, I'd encourage you to treat this book as I have: as a focus for learning, as a beginning, rather than a static entity. A good starting point would be to write your own short, personalised definitions of what it means to be Authentic, Responsible and Courageous. After all, my intent here was to get you thinking so you could challenge yourself then make these words your own:

Authentic

Responsible

Courageous

---

2. Mastery is pain

As we've already seen, living up to these three words isn't easy. It takes effort and practice over a long period of time. It requires us to make mistakes along the way, which some say is the only evidence that we're doing something different. How we treat ourselves, and others, when we fail also says a lot about our mindset – not to mention our authenticity, responsibility and courage.

Failures and pain aside, mastery is also associated with 'flow' experiences – those fantastic moments where we're working almost unconsciously in situations where we're perfectly matched to the challenge at hand. We can learn a lot from those times when we've been in flow, when the dance has worked perfectly and naturally for us.

3. Mastery is an 'asymptote'

This word has its origins in geometry, where it refers to a curve that reaches out to a line but never quite touches it.

It contains two messages where ARC is concerned. Firstly, it echoes the notion of the dance and the importance of holding back from embracing one of the three qualities at the expense of the other two. Mastering the dance requires us to work on all three at once, constantly rising above the pull of these competing forces, finding ways 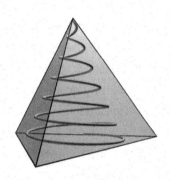 for them to complement each other. Rather than clinging to one face and trying to reach the top, we maintain a curved ascent up the inside of the pyramid, never touching the sides.

The second message is Daniel Pink's own meaning of the term asymptote as it relates to mastery. He says there is no end to mastery: it is a journey, a process, not a destination. Although we may get better and better at the dance, we can never reach the top of the pyramid. Our efforts in the dance take us spiralling upwards and upwards inside the pyramid, getting closer and closer to that elusive capstone, but – like the asymptote – our curve never reaches the line. There will always be room for improvement.

John Donahoe summed it up when he was President of eBay:

"Leadership is a journey, not a destination. It is a marathon, not a sprint. It is a process, not an outcome." [240]

For leaders like Donahoe, the capstone of the ARC pyramid is an aspiration, a holy grail. It's the reason we're on the journey. It's the direction we're headed. It's not the destination. That doesn't mean there aren't clear markers on the way. There are degrees of authenticity, degrees of responsibility and degrees of courage. Different people are operating at different levels when it comes to the dance. But that's another story…

The journey up this pyramid is a personal journey, as well as a professional one, for as Warren Bennis once said, "The process of becoming a leader is much the same as the process of becoming an integrated human being."[241]

Being on this journey means being wholeheartedly committed to all three qualities, while at the same time unattached to any single one of them. Staying on the journey means taking stock from time to time – asking ourselves questions like "Am I still on the journey or taking a detour?" and "Am I dancing, or caught in a corner?" The higher we rise inside the pyramid, the more we're able to feel centred whilst still being in flux and the more we come to realise that "I *am* the dance, not the dancer". Now, if that sounds a bit 'new age', it's because it's a similar message to ones taught in Taoism, Sufism and the Noble Eightfold Path of Buddhism – which, of course, are very much 'old age' but have stood the test of time.

Five final, practical tips to help you make the most of this book

As we've already seen, being Authentic, Responsible and Courageous won't be easy but it will pay dividends. To some extent, the fact that it *is* difficult makes the journey all the more valuable and it is a way to differentiate yourself from the rest of the pack. But, once you've started the dance – and shown others you're committed to it – you'll see it gets easier. Once they know what you're aiming for, your friends and colleagues will respect your commitment and – most of them at least – will support you, in your successes and in your increasingly infrequent failures.

These five final tips are intended to increase your chances of success. Not all of them will make your life easier, but they're all worth the effort.

1. Start with tangible, meaningful and achievable goals

Every journey needs a route, even if that initial route doesn't take us much further than the end of the street. The three ARC qualities work really well reactively – I run all my big decisions through the ARC test. They're even more powerful, though, when we apply them *proactively*.

The clearest way to do this is to apply them to your core tasks as a leader. However complex your world is, there are essentially three things you need to achieve for your team and/or your organisation. You need to Establish a Direction; Secure the Commitment of your team and stakeholders; and Build the Capacity within and around the team in order to get where you need to go. You also need to apply these Three Core Disciplines of Leadership to yourself, which means having a sense of your own Direction, maintaining your Commitment and continually working on your own Capacity to deliver.

Boston's Three Core Disciplines of Leadership

ESTABLISH DIRECTION

SELF

TEAM

ORGANISATION

SECURE COMMITMENT

BUILD CAPACITY

The ARC qualities offer a mindset that enables us to deliver against these Three Core Disciplines in a way that's more effective, sustainable and inspiring.

To ensure the time you've invested in this book actually makes a difference, I'd encourage you to set one ARC goal against each of 2-3 Core Disciplines. By way of example…

- I'll Establish a Direction for my team that is bold, true to what I believe in, and addresses the needs of the entire system that the team exists to support

- I'll more effectively Secure Commitment from my team and our stakeholders by connecting more authentically with them and creating a sense of common purpose – something that stretches us and that we're all committed to taking responsibility for

- I'll Build my organisation's Capacity by role-modelling the courage required to make mistakes and 'unlearn' outdated ways of doing things; by being honest about my own failings, shortcomings and development needs; by ensuring continuous improvement is every-body's responsibility.

2. Manage your own expectations – and those of others

Managing our own expectations itself takes authenticity, responsibility and courage. For instance, far too many people fall foul of 'false hope syndrome'[242]. With all the best intentions, we imagine a better future for ourselves (and perhaps others) and we vow to make the necessary changes to make that future a reality. Hearing the promise, our brain releases a trickle of neurotransmitters to reward us, our pre-frontal cortex decides its job is done and we get back to business as usual. No action follows. Nothing changes. We file the commitment away in the bottom drawer of a cabinet full of well meant but ultimately empty promises.

Beware false hope. But also be wary of the power of our own immune systems and those of the world around us. As we've already discussed, any new idea or behaviour will probably be met with resistance of some kind – from ourselves, our loved ones and the ones we don't really love all that much. Once you have your goal, look back at the network of responsibilities you identified in Part 3. How will this affect *them*? And how can you help the system adapt to (even welcome) the change?

3. Consider making your goal, or the qualities themselves, part of your identity

As we saw in Chapter 16, identity is a powerful tool for change. If I think I'm lazy, I'll find it much harder to meet my deadlines. The more I tell myself I'm disorganised, the less organised I become. In reality, the chances are I'm sometimes lazy, sometimes not; sometimes organised, sometimes not. The behaviours themselves are just that: behaviours.

If you're worried I'm asking you to change something fundamental about yourself, then think of it as a trick. There's no cult here, just a means of increasing the likelihood that you'll deliver on your own aspirations. Try telling yourself you're Courageous – that those times when you haven't displayed courage were blips, behavioural aberrations driven by the circumstances in which you found yourself. It will make a small difference at first, nothing huge. Maybe you'll speak up in a meeting where you'd previously have stayed quiet. But you *will* start to see progress. Once you do, tell yourself you're Courageous *and* Responsible. Then, when that makes a noticeable difference, introduce authenticity as a part of your identity. It'll be easier than the other two, because – thanks to them – you'll have been living it more already.

When being Authentic, Responsible and Courageous becomes a part of our identity, the three qualities become so much more accessible. They're no longer quite as difficult, no longer lofty ideals we struggle to live up to.

4. Monitor your progress

Do it every day – once a month or once a week rarely work. A score out of 10 on each of the three qualities is enough to maintain the momentum. But make sure you keep a record of your scores. This enables you to do two simple but effective things: calculate your average weekly score across all three qualities (a score out of 30), and aim to increase it by 1-2 points each week – a target that may seem small but has the benefits of making a noticeable difference while still being maintainable over time.

Of course, if you can monitor your progress to a greater level of detail it will dramatically increase your chances of success. Similarly, monitoring is easier if we seek feedback from others. It's for that reason that my colleagues and I are currently developing a means of measuring authenticity, responsibility and courage that will help leaders and their teams gauge their progress when it comes to demonstrating each of the three ARC qualities. But that's not the only way to closely monitor progress. If you *can* make the time, reflect on what works and what doesn't. Revisit some of the questions in this book. Revisit those chapters that highlight the reasons each quality is essential and the reasons that quality is hard to maintain. Remind yourself that this is a journey, a dance that's sometimes uncomfortable, always challenging, but brings rich rewards.

5. Make it social

Role models can be an enormous asset. So can the people to whom you made your commitments in Chapters 7, 12 and 18. The more you share your goal and talk about it, the more encouragement and support you'll get – the more people you can turn to when you suffer setbacks and when you're worried a setback is on its way.

But 'making it social' isn't a one-way affair. The more you talk about your goal, the more it will infect others. If it's Authentic, Responsible and Courageous it will appeal to far more people than just you. And be sure to make it social when you succeed. Remember Courage Blindness?

Remember all those reasons you and others have for not being Authentic, Responsible and Courageous? If people see and hear about you doing it, they'll be far more likely to try it themselves.

I've done this myself. I've shared my commitment with friends, colleagues and clients – some of whom have come back to me with their own examples of using ARC in their life (big and small; in and outside of work). And I've tried to role-model the three qualities for my daughter – in the ethical decisions I've made in her presence and the choices we've made together. I don't use the words, but the ethos is there.

Making it social is how we really get this to work.

• ● •

Conclusion

Back in the 1990s, Bill George, author of *True North*, observed many of the wrong people being chosen to run corporations. "Under pressure from Wall Street to maximize short-term earnings, boards of directors frequently chose leaders for their charisma instead of their character, their style rather than their substance, and their image instead of their integrity."[243]

It's pretty much the same today, and things won't change themselves. Take a moment to picture the world we'll create if we continue on this trajectory. It's a world run by people who consistently prioritise themselves over others; people whose principles and values are buried so deeply they never see the light of day. Imagine a world where you never really know who your colleagues are or what they stand for; a world where people put up with all manner of atrocities because they're afraid to challenge the status quo – or feel they don't have the time, skills or right to take a stand. Imagine a world where authenticity, responsibility and courage are the stuff of fiction – or, worse, they're words on a wall or the cover of a book that are proudly displayed but rarely lived up to. What kind of organisation would you be working in? What would it be like in your team? How would you feel at the start of each day as you headed in to work, and at the end of the week when you headed back home?

Now imagine the opposite: a world where leaders are chosen for their ability to act authentically, responsibly and courageously. Imagine a world run by people who are consistently true to themselves and their values; who don't pretend to be someone else in order to progress their careers; who stand up for what is right rather than keeping their heads down and protecting their own interests. Imagine what it would be like if you and the leaders around you challenged yourselves to invest your privileges in making a difference at a local, national and/or global level – contributing significantly more to society than each of you is taking from it.

I believe the world deserves leaders that we can be proud to follow. And I'm hoping I've left you with a concept that is simple to grasp but enables you to explore yourself and your leadership at considerable depth. I hope you find the idea of being Authentic, Responsible and Courageous as compelling as it is challenging. The world needs its leaders to step up. It needs them to stand for something worthwhile. It needs leaders who are focused on harnessing and enhancing our increasing interdependence, not leaders who are determined to ignore or exploit it. We need leaders we can believe in – not just at the top of organisations, but all the way up. We need leaders who will do what's right in spite of all the pressures to do otherwise.

It may not be easy, but whatever our starting points, we are all capable of doing this. As you consider what you'll do differently as a result of reading this book, I'd ask you to reflect on the following words...

You might start big
You might start small
But what will your life amount to
If you never start at all?

Appendices

Values exercise
(Chapters 4, 11 and 17)

ON THE FOLLOWING PAGES is a list of values, in alphabetical order. Your

goal is to use this list to populate the two tables below. You can use whatever method you like, but the following method typically gets the best results:

1. Start with the 'Most important to me' table

2. Pick seven values for each of the two columns (Terminal and Instrumental values[244]) and write them in, remembering to…

   a. take your time

   b. finish the 'Terminal values' column before moving to the next column

   c. do not rank them at this point

4. Cross off two from each column – again, take your time

5. Rank those that remain in order of their importance to you (1-5 in each of the Terminal and Instrumental columns – where 1 is 'most important')

   a. take your time over this and think carefully

   b. feel free to change your rankings (or values) as often as you like

3. Move to the 'Least important to me' table and pick five values for each column – be honest with yourself, as we cannot all value everything

4. Cross off two from each column, then rank those that remain in order of their importance to you (1-3 in each of the two columns – where 1 is 'least important')

5. Reflect on the questions that follow

Most important to me

Rank	Terminal values *What I want to achieve in life (i.e. my destination in life)*	Rank	Instrumental values *How I want to achieve it (i.e. the way in which I want to travel to my destination)*

Least important to me

Rank	Terminal values	Rank	Instrumental values

For each column (Terminal and Instrumental Values) ask yourself…

1. Why are the top three my top three?

2. When has my adherence to these values really been challenged?

3. How do I embody these values as a leader?

4. What impact does my choice of bottom three have on my leadership?

Values – some examples

Feel free to add your own.

You will find some of these values very similar, but subtly different. This is intentional.

Accountability	Achievement	Advancement
Ambition	Arts	Authenticity
Balance (of…?)	Beauty	Being admired
Being liked	Change	Clarity
Collaboration	Comfort	Commercial success
Commitment	Community	Compassion
Competence	Contentment	Continuous learning
Contribution	Co-operation	Courage
Creativity	Culture	Dependability
Discipline	Efficiency	Enthusiasm
Environment	Equality	Ethics
Excellence	Excitement	Fairness
Family	Financial gain	Forgiveness
Freedom	Friendships	Future generations

Generosity	Growth	Harmony
Health	Helping others	Honesty
Humility	Humour/fun	Inclusion
Independence	Influence	Initiative
Innovation	Integrity	Intelligence
Interdependence	Intuition	Involvement
Job security	Leadership	Listening
Location	Logic	Love
Loyalty	Making a difference	Meaningful work
Mission focus	Obedience	Open communication
Open-mindedness	Openness	Order/structure
Peace (at a global level)	Peace (at a personal level)	Perseverance
Personal fulfilment	Personal growth	Physical fitness
Physical pleasure	Politeness	Power
Privacy	Quality	Recognition
Relationships	Religion	Reputation
Respect	Responsibility	Risk taking
Safety	Security	Self confidence
Self discipline	Simplicity	Spirituality
Stability	Status	Success
Sustainability	Tidiness	Tolerance
Trust	Truth	Variety
Vision	Wealth	Wisdom

References
and endnotes

• ● •

1. Words uttered by King Henry IV in Shakespeare's Henry IV (Part II Act 3, Scene 1).

2. The actual words are "Leadership is a poison except to the one who possesses the antidote in his heart". See Mevlana Jalal al-din Rumi's *Mathnawi II*, 3464.

3. See page 64 of P. Hawkins (2005) *Wise Fool's Guide to Leadership: Short spiritual stories for organisational and personal Transformation*. London: O Books.

4. Quoted on page 28 of P. Hawkins (2014, 2nd edition) *Leadership Team Coaching: Developing Collective Transformational Leadership*. London: Kogan Page.

5. From page xiii of B. George (with P. Sims) (2007) *True North*. San Francisco, California: Jossey-Bass.

6. From personal communications with Professor Peter Hawkins.

7. The idea of a 'Developed World' and a 'Developing World' is a nonsense: even those nations who would rather stand still have been forced to evolve by changes in the world around them. Whether you're an individual or a country, considering yourself 'developed' is a dangerous fallacy.

8. Data provided by ITU World Telecommunication in July 2012.

9. Adapted from page 171 of R. Heifetz, A. Grashow & M. Linsky (2009) *The Practice of Adaptive Leadership: tools and tactics for changing your organisation and the world*. Boston, Massachusetts: Harvard Business Press.

10. J. Board, C. Bones, S. Lee, K. Money & B. Scott-Quinn (2009) The Henley Manifesto: Restoring Confidence and Trust in UK PLC. Retrieved from www. henley.reading.ac.uk/web/FILES/corporate/cl-White_Paper_Henley_Manifesto_ Chris_Bones.pdf on 26 March 2012.

11. From page 131 of J.S. Mill (1848) *Principles of Political Economy*. London: John W. Parker.

12. These data come from the Edelman Trust Barometer (2011, 2012 and 2013). You'll find the various surveys at www.edelman.com.

13. See the Edelman Trust Barometer from 2013 at www.edelman.com.

14. Board, Bones, Lee, Money & Scott-Quinn (2009) *op. cit.*

15. *Ibid.*

16. D. Halpern (2005) Trust in business and trust between citizens. Prime Minister's Strategy Unit, April 13. Cited in S.M.R. Covey & R. R. Merrill (2006) *The Speed of Trust: The One Thing that Changes Everything.* New York: Simon & Schuster.

17. Edelman trust barometer 2012: informed public's trust in NGOs (51-30; 50% for general public). See www.edelman.com.

18. Board, Bones, Lee, Money & Scott-Quinn (2009) *op. cit.,* p.18.

19. J. N. Drobak, John N. (1998) Law Matters. Washington University *Law Quarterly, 76(1),* 97-104.

20. I've drawn on several sources for this, but have added 'common ground' and the extent to which 'you' trust 'them'. Sources include V. Hope-Hailey, R. Searle & G. Dietz (2012) Organisational effectiveness: How trust helps. *People Management,* 28 February 2012 (available from www.peoplemanagement.co.uk/pm/articles/ 2012/02/organisational-effectiveness-how-trust-helps.htm); V. Hope-Hailey, R. Searle & G. Dietz (2012) *Where has all the trust gone? CIPD Research Report, March 2012.* London: Chartered Institute of Personnel and Development; D.L. Ferrin (2012) *On the Rise and Fall of Trust ...and the Continuing Rise of Trust Research.* CS Myers Lecture at the annual conference of the British Psychological Society's Division of Occupational Psychology, 14 January.

21. See page 12 of V. Hope-Hailey, R. Searle & G. Dietz (2012) *Where has all the trust gone? CIPD Research Report, March 2012.* London: Chartered Institute of Personnel and Development.

22. Retrieved from http://shifthappens.wikispaces.com/ on 26 February 2013.

23. Taken from page 54 of J. L. Badaracco, Jr. (2002) *Leading Quietly: an unorthodox guide to doing the right thing.* Boston, Massachusetts: Harvard Business School Press.

24. C. Thompson (2007) The see-through CEO. *Wired Magazine, 15 (4),* March (Retrieved from www.wired.com/wired/archive/15.04/wired40_ceo.html on 29 July 2012).

25. Harris Interactive (2005) *The Harris Poll,* #4, 13 January. Cited in Covey & Merrill (2006) *op. cit.*

26. KPMG (2000) Organizational Integrity Survey. Washington, DC: KPMG. Cited in S.M.R. Covey & R. R. Merrill (2006) *The Speed of Trust: The One Thing that Changes Everything.* New York: Simon & Schuster.

27. *Ibid.*

28. M. Kohn (2008) *Trust: self-interest and the common good.* New York: Oxford

University Press Inc.

29. In the UK and the rest of northwest Europe, distrust in the Police is still less than 20%. Distrust runs to almost 40% in Poland, France and Hungary; over 40% in Bulgaria and the Czech Republic; and exceeds 60% in Russia. From an ongoing programme by the London School of Economics entitled *Trust in the Police and Criminal Courts: A Comparative European Analysis* available at www2.lse.ac.uk/methodologyInstitute/whosWho/Jackson/jackson_ESS.aspx.

30. Cited in Covey & Merrill (2006) *op. cit.*

31. D.L. McCabe, K.D. Butterfield & L.K. Treviño (2006) Academic Dishonesty in Graduate Business Programs: Prevalence, Causes, and Proposed Action, *Academy of Management Learning & Education*, 2006, Vol. 5, No. 3, 294–305. The study is based on survey responses from 5,331 students at 32 graduate schools in the United States and Canada.

32. F. Sierles, I. Hendrickx & S. Circle (1980) Cheating in Medical School. *Journal of Medical Education, 55 (2)*, 124-25.

33. M. Ransford (1999) *Convicts and MBA Grads Have Similar Ethics.* Ball State University. Cited in S.M.R. Covey & R. R. Merrill (2006) *The Speed of Trust: The One Thing that Changes Everything.* New York: Simon & Schuster.

34. The sample included 527 MBA students. See Hill & Knowlton (2008) *Reputation and the War for Talent.* From Hill & Knowlton's Corporate Reputation Watch series.

35. D.L. McCabe (2009) MBAs Cheat. But Why? *Harvard Business Review Blog*, 13 April. Retrieved from http://blogs.hbr.org/how-to-fix-business-schools/2009/04/mbas-cheat-but-why.html on 26 February 2013.

36. McCabe, Butterfield & Treviño (2006) *op. cit.*

37. Walumbwa, Fred; Avolio, Bruce; Gardner, William; Wernsing, Tara; and Peterson (2008) *Authentic Leadership: Development and Validation of a Theory-Based Measure.* Management Department Faculty Publications. Paper 24.

38. B.J. Avolio & W.L. Gardner (2005) Authentic Leadership Development: Getting to the root of positive forms of leadership. *Leadership Quarterly, 16,* 315-338; and B. George (2003) *Authentic Leadership: Rediscovering the secrets to creating lasting value.* San Francisco: Jossey-Bass. Cited in Walumbwa, Avolio, Gardner, Wernsing & Peterson (2008) *op. cit.*

39. The argument runs like this: authentic leaders are transparent when dealing with challenges. So the process by which followers internalize their beliefs and values is probably based less on inspirational appeals, dramatic presentations, symbolism, or other forms of impression management – see W.L. Gardner &

B.J. Avolio (1998) The charismatic relationship: A dramaturgical perspective. *Academy of Management Review, 23,* 32-58. Walumbwa et al (2008) compared authentic leadership with transformational leadership and ethical leadership. They found that Authentic leadership alone lacks the inspirational motivation that's at the heart of transformational leadership. This problem is addressed, I believe, by mixing in Courage and Responsibility. See Walumbwa, Avolio, Gardner, Wernsing & Peterson (2008) *op. cit.*

40. H. Harung, F. Travis, W. Blank & D. Heaton (2009) Higher development, brain integration, and excellence in leadership. *Management Decision, 47 (6),* 872-894. They also cite evidence from J.C. Collins & J.I. Porras (2002) *Built To Last: Successful habits of visionary companies.* New York, NY: Harper Business Essential.

41. J. Collins (2001) *Good to Great: Why some companies make the leap... and others don't.* London: Random House.

42. Kernis, M. H. 2003. Toward a conceptualization of optimal self-esteem. *Psychological Inquiry, 14*: 1-26.

43. Based on 2011 figures from his profile on Forbes, retrieved from www.forbes.com/profile/david-dillon/ on 20 June 2012.

44. From page xxxiv of B. George (with P. Sims) (2007) *True North.* San Francisco, California: Jossey-Bass.

45. E. Kennedy-Moore & J. C. Watson (2001) How and when does emotional expression help? *Review of General Psychology, 5,* 187-212. Cited in D. Goleman (2006) *Social intelligence.* New York: Random House, Inc.

46. A. A. Grandey, G.M. Fisk, A.S. Mattila, K.J. Jansen & L.A. Sideman (2005) Is "service with a smile" enough? Authenticity of positive displays during service encounters. *Organizational Behavior and Human Decision Processes, 96*: 38-55.

47. M.H. Kernis (2003) Toward a conceptualization of optimal self-esteem. *Psychological Inquiry, 14*: 1-26.

48. Sloane was a long-term friend of George H.W. Bush, an ex-CIA case officer turned peace activist, who became a Presbyterian Minister and chaplain of Williams College and Yale University. The quote is commonly attributed Lily Tomlin (actress, comedian, writer, and producer) who used it in People magazine (26 Dec 1977) but is cited as Sloane's in F.R. Shapiro (2006) *The Yale Book of Quotations.* Yale University Press.

49. From page 81 of S. Scott (2009) *Fierce Leadership: a bold alternative to the worst 'best practices' of business today.* London: Piatkus.

50. Quote taken from page 186 of B.M. Bass & P. Steidlmeier (1999). Ethics, character,

and authentic transformational leadership behavior. *Leadership Quarterly, 10*, 181-217. Cited in Walumbwa, Avolio, Gardner, Wernsing & Peterson (2008) *op. cit.*

51. R. Goffee and G. Jones (2000) *Why should anyone be led by you?* Harvard Business Review, Sept-Oct.

52. The essence of some of the input from participants on my own ARC Leadership Programme.

53. P. Aitken (Date unknown) *Five routes to 'Real' Leadership Development.* Henley white paper, retrieved from www.henley.reading.ac.uk/web/FILES/corporate/cl-White_Paper_Five_routes_to_Real_Leadership_Development_P_Atkin.pdf on 26 March 2012.

54. R.M. Ryan & E.L Deci (2003). On assimilating identities to the self: A self-determination theory perspective on internalization and integrity within cultures. In M. R. Leary & J. P. Tangney (Eds.) *Handbook of self and identity,* pp 253-272. New York: Guilford. Cited in Walumbwa, Avolio, Gardner, Wernsing & Peterson (2008) *op. cit.*

55. Adapted from Carl Rogers on congruence Rogers, C.R. (1961/1967) *On Becoming a Person: A Therapist's View of Psychotherapy.* London: Constable.

56. P. Hawkins & C. Smith (2011) Two steps to Success. *The Training Journal,* February.

57. *Ibid.*

58. *Ibid.*

59. S. Harter (2002) Authenticity. *In C. R. Snyder & S. J. Lopez (Eds.), Handbook of positive psychology:* 382-394. London: Oxford University Press. Cited in Walumbwa, Avolio, Gardner, Wernsing & Peterson (2008) *op. cit.*

60. A. Paulos (2006) The self is a conceptual chimera. In J. Brockman (ed) *What is your dangerous idea?* p154. London: Simon & Schuster.

61. Quoted from page 102 of D. Goleman (1998) *Vital Lies, Simple Truths: The Psychology Of Self-Deception.* London: Bloomsbury.

62. OPP (2007) *Who's fooling whom? Exploring the impact of impression management in the workplace.* Oxford Psychologists Press, research report.

63. Baumeister, R. F. (1982) A self-presentational view of social phenomena. *Psychological Bulletin, 91,* 3-26.

64. R. Zinko, G.R. Ferris, S.E. Humphrey, C.J. Meyer & F. Aime (2012) Personal reputation in organizations: Two-study constructive replication and extension of antecedents and consequences. *Journal of Occupational and Organizational Psychology, 85,* 156-180.

65. For example, the research behind two reputable psychometrics: Will Schutz's FIRO-B and the Myers-Briggs Type Indicator.

66. The formulation of this question and the next is partly inspired by one of many fantastic books that have enhanced my work as a coach: R. Kegan & L. Lahey (2009) *Immunity to Change: How to overcome it and unlock the potential in yourself and your organization.* Harvard Business School Press.

67. Kegan & Lahey (2009) *op. cit.*

68. R.E. Kelly (1985) *The Gold-Collar Worker: Harnessing the brainpower of the new workforce.* Reading,MA: Addison Wesley.

69. Harung, Travis, Blank & Heaton (2009) *op. cit.*

70. Electroencephelograms (EEGs) used as part of the development of a Brain Integration Scale.

71. Stated by Harung, Travis, Blank & Heaton (2009) *op. cit.*

72. See, for example R.A. Baer (2003) Mindfulness training as a clinical intervention: A conceptual and empirical review. *Clinical Psychology: Science and Practice, 10 (2),* 125-143; JM Greeson (2009) Mindfulness research update 2008. *Complementary Health Practice Review, 14 (1),* 10-18.

73. Stated by Harung, Travis, Blank & Heaton (2009) *op. cit.*

74. For example L Visu-Petra, L Cheie, O Benga, M Miclea (2011) Cognitive control goes to school. *Procedia – Social and Behavioural Sciences, 11,* 240-244.

75. R. Wolever, K. Bobinet, K. McCabe, E. Mackenzie, E. Fekete, C. Kusnick & M. Baime (2012) Effective and viable mind-body stress reduction in the workplace: A randomized controlled trial. *Journal of Occupational Health Psychology, 17 (2),* 246-258.

76. P. Lally, C. van Jaarsveld, H. Potts & J. Wardle (2010). How are habits formed? Modelling habit formation in the real world. *European Journal of Social Psychology, 40 (6),* 998-1009.

77. From page 154 of George (with Sims) (2007) *op. cit.*

78. I think I created this (in 2008), but I have to confess I'm not entirely sure. I certainly gave it the name!

79. The term is typically spelt with a 'z' as its originator was an American psychologist, Abraham Maslow.

80. Yes, I know, it wasn't until the 1950s that the theory was fully expressed in print – see A. Maslow (1954). *Motivation and personality.* Harper and Row New York, New York.

81. See, for example, M. Newman (2008) *Emotional Capitalists: The new leaders.*

Chichester, W. Sussex: John Wiley & Sons.

82. D. T. Kenrick, V. Griskevicius, S. L. Neuberg & M. Schaller (2010) Renovating the Pyramid of Needs: Contemporary Extensions Built Upon Ancient Foundations. *Perspectives on Psychological Science, 5 (3)*, 292-314.

83. In S. Cook-Greuter (1999) *Postautonomous Ego Development: its nature and measurement.* Doctoral dissertation. Cambridge, MA: Harvard Graduate School of Education. Cited in H. Harung, F. Travis, W. Blank, D. Heaton (2009) Higher development, brain integration, and excellence in leadership. *Management Decision, 47 (6)*, 872-894.

84. Inspired by a number of sources, including J. Rogers (2008) *Coaching Skills: A Handbook.* Open University Press; Newman (2008) *op. cit.* Chichester, W. Sussex: John Wiley & Sons; and S.J. Stein & H.E. Book (2000) *The EQ Edge: Emotional intelligence and your success.* Toronto: Multi-Health Systems Inc.

85. Personal communication: Peter once encouraged me to do the same exercise.

86. F. Schulz von Thun (2005) *Miteinander reden 1: Störungen und Klärungen. Allgemeine Psychologie der Kommunikation.* Reinbek, Germany: Rowohlt Taschenbuch Verla.

87. D. Dunning, K. Johnson, J. Ehrlinger & J. Kruger (2003). Why people fail to recognize their own incompetence. *Current Directions in Psychological Science, 12 (3)*, 83–87. Found thanks to http://en.wikipedia.org/wiki/Illusory_superiority#Notes (Retrieved on 9 April 2012).

88. H.H. Meyer (1980). Self-appraisal of job performance. *Personnel Psychology, 33*, 291-95.

89. D. Goleman, R. Boyatzis & A. McKee (2002) *The New Leaders: Transforming the art of leadership into the science of results.* London: Little, Brown.

90. The majority of men have a 'Thinking' preference in Myers-Briggs terms (Myers-Briggs, or MBTI, being a way of looking at personality). I was told when I first qualified in MBTI that Thinking types tend to prefer their feedback to come from above. I've since tested this myself with hundreds of people in various organisations – albeit most of them Europeans.

91. S. A. Snook (2000). *Friendly Fire: The Accidental Shootdown of U.S. Black Hawks over Northern Iraq.* Princeton, NJ: Princeton University Press. The quote is taken from page 135. For more information on this incident and the Air Force Regulation 110-14 accident investigation report, either read Snook's book or go to http://en.wikipedia.org/wiki/1994_Black_Hawk_shootdown_incident (Retrieved on 9 April 2012)

92. Young and Rubicam is a commercial communications network with 6500 people

in 90 countries. This quote comes from page 164 of George (with Sims) (2007) *op. cit.*

93. In a 2011 survey of medium-to-large UK-headquartered companies, 61% of managers said senior leadership had become more short-term oriented. In organisations with 10,000+ employees, the3 figure rose to 88%. Figures from J. Cowell (2012) *UK Leadership – Stuck in a crisis mentality?* Webinar, 20 March 2012. Research based on a survey of 201 managers in medium to large UK-headquartered businesses.

94. These figures are taken from G. Pearson, P. Wilton and P. Woodman (2011) *Economic Outlook, Issue 5 (October).* UK Chartered Management Institute (CMI) report. As the report's Introduction states, the CMI "invited 15,000 of its members to complete an online survey between 1-19 September 2011. A total of 616 responses were received from across the UK, drawn from industry sectors across the economy and from managers at a range of levels of seniority up to directors and chief executives."

95. Cowell (2012) *op. cit.*

96. From a presentation at 2011's annual conference of the British Psychological Society's Division of Occupational Psychology, by Professor Cary L. Cooper, CBE, who is Distinguished Professor of Organizational Psychology and Health at the UK's Lancaster University.

97. *Ibid.*

98. A. Oswald (2002) Are You Happy at Work? Job Satisfaction and Work-Life Balance in the US and Europe. Paper presented at the *Warwick Business School event*, on 5 November 2002 at the Warwick Hotel, New York. Oswald is Professor of Economics at the University of Warwick in the UK.

99. *Ibid.*

100. There's no one reference I'd cite here. Not even half a dozen could do the research justice. Take a look at any of the UK's Health and Safety Executive reports or the work of Cary Cooper and you'll get the idea.

101. V. Hope-Hailey, R. Searle & G. Dietz (2012) *Where Has All The Trust Gone? CIPD Research Report, March 2012.* London: Chartered Institute of Personnel and Development.

102. B. Kellerman (2008) *Followership: How.* Harvard Business School Press.

103. B. Ware (2012) *Top Five Regrets of the Dying – A Life Transformed by the Dearly Departing.* London: Hay House.

104. When I read these Top 5 Regrets, I do wonder whether we should live our lives

beholden to those last few minutes. There's such a huge shift in perspective when we're looking death in the face. We're suddenly confronted with a way of thinking that's so different to the "rules" by which we've made the vast majority of our daily decisions in life. It's a profoundly unique experience. But are those dying minutes, days or weeks really more important than any other minutes, days or weeks in our lives? Are we really any wiser? Or, faced with the stark reality of our mortality, are we closer in nature to animals than we've been since we were children? Just a little food for thought!

105. Oswald (2002) *op. cit.* I have used 'UK' rather than 'Great Britain' for the sake of consistency in this book, but I recognise that the data set excludes Northern Ireland.

106. During a 'question and answer' session at a leadership conference for one of my clients, in Miami, Florida in 2010. Clinton was a guest speaker. I was a facilitator.

107. From page 187 of Heifetz, Grashow & Linsky (2009) *op. cit.*

108. These figures are taken from G. Pearson, P. Wilton and P. Woodman (2011) *Economic Outlook, Issue 5 (October).* Chartered Management Institute report (CMI). As the report's Introduction states, the CMI "invited 15,000 of its members to complete an online survey between 1-19 September 2011. A total of 616 responses were received from across the UK, drawn from industry sectors across the economy and from managers at a range of levels of seniority up to directors and chief executives."

109. From pages 208-9 of P. Senge, J. Jaworski, C. Scharmer & B. Flowers (2005) *Presence: Exploring Profound Change in People, Organizations and Society.* Nicholas Brealey.

110. B. Ewing, D. Moore, S. Goldfinger, A. Oursler, A. Reed & M. Wackernagel (2010) *The Ecological Footprint Atlas 2010.* Oakland: Global Footprint Network.

111. This quote is taken from page 298 of H. Gardner (2006) Following Sisyphus. In J. Brockman (ed) *What is your dangerous idea?* p298-9. London: Simon & Schuster.

112. It's a term coined by Denise Rousseau, who has been a professor at universities in UK, USA, Singapore, Thailand and China and has authored at least 10 books and over 160 research articles. Read more about Denise Rousseau at www. heinz.cmu.edu/faculty-and-research/faculty-profiles/faculty-details/index. aspx?faculty_id=81 (Retrieved on 16 July 2012).

113. M. Sandel (2012) *What Money Can't Buy: The Moral Limits of Markets.* Allen Lane.

114. Myers-Briggs Type Indicator, MBTI® and its logo are registered trademarks of

the Myers-Briggs Type Indicator Trust.

115. A.I. Jack, A.J. Dawson, K.L. Begany, R.L. Leckie, K.P. Barry, A.H. Ciccia & A.Z. Snyder (2013) fMRI reveals reciprocal inhibition between social and physical cognitive domains. *Neurolmage, 66,* 385–401.

116. S. Baron-Cohen (2006). A political system based on empathy. In J. Brockman (ed) *What is your dangerous idea?* p208-10. London: Simon & Schuster. Simon Baron-Cohen is not to be confused with his cousin Sacha, famous (or infamous) for controversial characters like Ali G, Borat and Bruno.

117. From page 209 of S. Baron-Cohen (2006) *op. cit.*

118. Cited on page 184 of A. Cohen (1949) *Everyman's Talmud*. New York: Schocken. I'd come across this statement before (my grandfather was Jewish) but was inspired to include it here when I saw it on page 34 of Badaracco, Jr. (2002) *op. cit.*

119. For this and other amusing mistakes on a similar theme, see 'Doing a Ratner' and other famous gaffes. *The Telegraph,* 22 December 2007 (Author's name not cited). Retrieved from www.telegraph.co.uk/news/uknews/1573380/Doing-a-Ratner-and-other-famous-gaffes.html on 20 August 2012. Incidentally, one of my clients recently saw Ratner speak on a leadership programme. She said she found him "truly impressive" and that is was "amazing to hear his story from him and also the following darker chapters before he had the courage to step back into life and be where he is today."

120. One of several current examples discussed on a BBC radio show I took part in (John Darvall, BBC Radio Bristol, 9:00 Wednesday, 11th April 2012).

121. From case studies in Scott (2009) *op. cit.*

122. This action was part of its "social mission" to make future generations of Japanese youth proud of their history. Goleman (1998) *op. cit.*

123. Quoted on page 137 of George (with Sims) (2007) *op. cit.*

124. From page 326 of M. Nicoll (1952) *Psychological Commentaries, Volume I.* London: Vincent Stuart Ltd.

125. Sufism is an Islamic tradition with a mystical, gnostic or esoteric component that has existed for over a thousand years.

126. Peter Hawkins introduced me to *adab* when I shared the experience I had in Madrid.

127. From page 83 of D. Goleman (1999) *Working With Emotional Intelligence.* London: Bloomsbury.

128. R. A. Clarke (2004) *Against All Enemies: inside America's war on terror.* New York: Free Press. Cited in R. Heifetz, A. Grashow & M. Linsky (2009) *The Practice*

of Adaptive Leadership: tools and tactics for changing your organisation and the world. Boston, Massachusetts: Harvard Business Press.

129. A great starting point where 'hot buttons' are concerned is S. Evans & S. Suib Cohen (2000) *Hot Buttons: How to resolve conflict and cool everyone down.* London: Piatkus.

130. I've pulled these from various sources, originally for a book entitled *How To Be A Truly Dreadful Leader,* which I've yet to finish. I put it on hold to focus on this one.

131. See page 35 of Badaracco, Jr. (2002) *op. cit.*

132. This story is told in Badaracco, Jr. (2002) *op. cit.* It's one for which I've struggled to find any further detail.

133. Unnamed author (2012) The vanishing north. *The Economist, 16 June,* p13.

134. I'm grateful to Peter Hawkins for saying something about a tree in his garden, that reminded me of these things, which I'd long since left right at the back of on my mental 'backburner'. I'm glad they're now front of mind again.

135. These observations are influenced by page 45 of Badaracco, Jr. (2002) *op. cit.* Other influences here include Heifetz, Grashow & Linsky (2009) *op. cit.*; and Kegan & Lahey (2009) *op. cit.*

136. See page 323 of M. Heffernan (2012) *Willful Blindness: Why We Ignore the Obvious at Our Peril.* London: Simon & Schuster.

137. This is a story told in Goleman (1998) *op. cit.* He found it in S Sherman (1997) Levi's: As Ye Sew, So Shall Ye Reap. *Fortune magazine,* May 12, pp 104-116.

138. Lieutenant Colonel Krawchuk is quoted on page 329 of Heffernan (2012) *op. cit.*

139. R. Biswas-Diener (2012) *The Courage Quotient: How science can make you braver.* San Francisco, CA: Jossey-Bass.

140. If you don't know him, India Jones is a character played by Harrison Ford in four movies conceived originally by George Lucas and Steven Spielberg. Jones is an archaeologist who travels around the world having improbable, and incredibly brave adventures – and generally shows a lot of fear along the way!

141. From an interview with the author: A. Linley (2012) *The Courage Quotient with Dr. Robert Biswas-Diener (Part 2).* Retrieved from http://blog.cappeu.com/2012/04/10/the-courage-quotient-with-dr-robert-biswas-diener-part-1/?goback=%2Egde_3189061_member_106919936 on 18 June 2012.

142. Incidentally, this is a term I arrived at independently. Then I Googled the phrase, came across Susan Jeffers' book, read it and found common ground. Sadly, Susan died while I was writing my own book. 'Feel the fear and do it anyway' is a registered trademark. See S. Jeffers (2007) *Feel The Fear and Do It Anyway (20th anniversary edition).* London: Vermilion (Random House).

143. C. Peterson & M. E. P. Seligman (2004) *Character Strengths and Virtues: A Handbook and Classification*. OUP USA.

144. Biswas-Diener (2012) *op. cit.*, p9.

145. The author doesn't go into this level of detail as his is not that kind of book, but the behavioural activation system (BAS) is, the theory goes, made up of two subsystems – the dorsal striated and ventral. Overall, the BAS uses various structures including dopamine receptors in the midbrain. These send signals to the basal ganglia (the bunch of nerve cells at the bottom of the brain) and feed the sensory and motor cortices and the prefrontal cortex (otherwise known as the home of our 'executive function'). The behavioural inhibition system (BIS) uses the septo-hippocampal circuit which is primarily focused on memory and includes the hippocampus, dentate gyrus, entorhinal cortex and nerve cells that reach out to the pre-frontal cortex. If you'd like to read more, try J.A. Gray (1987) The neuropsychology of emotion and personality. In S.M. Stahl, S.D. Iverson & E.C. Goodman (Eds.) *Cognitive Neurochemistry*. Oxford: Oxford University Press; and/or J.A. Gray & N. McNaughton (2000) *The neuropsycholoogy of anxiety: an enquiry into the functions of the septo-hippocampal system*. Oxford: Oxford University Press.

146. Linley (2012) *op. cit.*

147. Thanks to Dan Goleman (2006) *op. cit.* for drawing my attention to S.S. Dickerson & M.E. Kemeny (2004) Acute stressors and cortisol responses: a theoretical integration and synthesis of laboratory research. *Psychological Bulletin, 130(3)*, 355-91.

148. The term 'psychological threat' isn't my first choice for the threats that remain. Social threats are psychological in nature and all fear is ultimately psychological. My personal, technical preference is 'intrapersonal' – I'd have called the social threats 'interpersonal'. But it's a technical distinction and 'intrapersonal' is, to many people, psychological jargon. Incidentally, I discovered while redrafting this book that the three types of threat loosely mirror Paul Tillich's three forms of anxiety (fear of death, of condemnation and of meaninglessness) as laid out in P. Tillich (2000) *The Courage To Be (2nd ed.)*. Yale University Press.

149. George (with Sims) (2007) *op. cit.,* p xxix

150. Field-Marshal Sir William Slim, Courage and other broadcasts, quoted on page 84 of the First edition (undated) of *Serve to lead (An anthology)*. The Royal Military Academy Sandhurst.

151. M. Hauser (2006) Our universal moral grammar's immunity to religion. In

J. Brockman (ed) *What is your dangerous idea?* London: Simon & Schuster. Pages 60-62.

152. From a definition of intellectual stimulation in Walumbwa, Avolio, Gardner, Wernsing & Peterson (2008) *op. cit.*

153. Adapted from Kegan & Lahey (2009) *op. cit.*

154. Heifetz, Grashow & Linsky (2009) *op. cit.*

155. I first came across this story in Heffernan (2012) *op. cit.*

156. See page 34 of Badaracco, Jr. (2002) *op. cit.*

157. I have to confess, I've really struggled to find the original source for this quote.

158. Biswas-Diener (2012) *op. cit.*, p27.

159. *Ibid.*, p10.

160. Heifetz, Grashow & Linsky (2009) *op. cit.*, p45.

161. JFK and Churchill are cited in Badaracco, Jr. (2002) *op. cit.* The comments about Nelson Mandela are drawn from A. Roberts (2008) Nelson Mandela is a hero, but not a saint. *The Guardian,* 26 June. Retrieved from www.guardian.co.uk/commentisfree/2008/jun/26/nelsonmandela.zimbabwe on 27 February 2013.

162. E.E. Shelp (1984) Courage: A neglected virtue in the patient-physician relationship. *Social Science and Medicine, 18,* 351-360. Cited in Peterson & Seligman (2004) *op. cit.*

163. B.J. Fowers (1998). Psychology And The Good Marriage: Social theory as practice. *American Behavioral Scientist, 41,* 516-541. Cited in Peterson & Seligman (2004) *op. cit.*

164. N. Way (1995) 'Can't You See The Courage, The Strength That I Have?' Listening to urban adolescent girls speak about their relationships. *Psychology of Women Quarterly, 19,* 107-128; and N. Way (1998) *Everyday Courage: the lives and stories of urban teenagers.* New York: New York University Press. Both cited Peterson & Seligman (2004) *op. cit.*

165. Political scientist Robert Axelrod set a bunch of computers to the task of identifying the optimal strategy back in the early 1970s – R. Axelrod (1985) *Evolution of co-operation.* New York: Basic.

166. Adapted from C. Argyris (1993) *Knowledge for Action.* San Francisco: Jossey-Bass.

167. George (with Sims) (2007) *op. cit.*, p xxiv.

168. Referenced in S. R. Covey's preface to J. M. Murdock & J. D. Ogden (2005) *Business with Integrity.* Utah: Brigham Young University.

169. From page 169 of A. De Mello (1997) *Awareness.* London: Fount Paperbacks.

170. *Ibid.*, p 70. Attributed to "An Italian poet" but I have been unable to track down the original source.
171. From page 434 of N. Stephenson (2008) *Anathem*. London: Atlantic Books.
172. Ware (2012) *op. cit.*
173. This is a question I've adapted slightly from page 174 of Scott (2009) *op. cit.*
174. These cases are all cited at one point or another in Heffernan (2012) *op. cit.*
175. *Ibid.* Steve Bolsin's words are taken from pages 285-6. His experiences are widely publicised and his actions led to a major government inquiry, which produced the *Kennedy Report* (available at www.bristol-inquiry.org.uk/final_report/index.htm) which itself had a massive influence on clinical governance in the UK.
176. This figure comes from a small but telling study including interviews with 40 MBA students, in F.J. Milliken, E.W. Morrison & P.F. Hewlin (2003) An exploratory study of employee silence: issues that employees don't communicate upward and why. *Journal of Management Studies, 40 (6)*, 1453-76.
177. This statistic is taken from research using Patrick Lencioni's Five Dysfunctions questionnaire. Across nearly 15,000 participants, they found that 68% of teams return a 'red' rating for Accountability. Executive teams comprised nearly 1,300 of those participants, and did far worse with 80% in the red. See: The Table Group (2006) *Online team assessment study reveals accountability crisis on [sic] teams.* Retrieved from www.tablegroup.com/about/press/release/?id=55 on 11 July 2012.
178. C.F. Alford (2001) *Whistle-blowers: broken lives and organizational power.* Ithaca: Cornell University Press.
179. Ethics Resource Center (2011) *National business ethics survey.* (Retrieved from www.ethics.org/nbes/files/FinalNBES-web.pdf on 16 July 2012).
180. See, for instance, Kohn (2008) *op. cit.* For studies of civil servants see I. Kawachi, B.P. Kennedy & R.G. Wilkinson (1999) *The society and population health reader, Volume 1: income inequality and health.* New York: New Press. For studies of similar phenomena in monkeys take a look at C. A. Shiveley & T.B. Clarkson (1994) Social status and coronary artery atherosclerosis in female monkeys. *Artereosclerosis and Thrombosis, 14,* 721-6.
181. I've read numerous references to this link between social interaction / isolation and incidences of cancer, in humans as well in laboratory mice. If you're interested, take a look at B.C. Trainor, C. Sweeney & R. Cardiff (2009) Isolating the Effects of Social Interactions on Cancer Biology. *Cancer Prevention Research, 2,* 843.
182. This quote comes from page 129 of Goleman (1999) *op. cit.*

183. G. Hofstede (2003) *Culture's Consequences: Comparing values, behaviors, insti-tutions and organizations across nations (2nd Edition).* London: Sage. Hofstede's research suggested that – at the time at least – the countries that were best able to tolerate ambiguity were Singapore, Jamaica, Denmark, Sweden and Hong Kong. Least able were Greece (and this was a long time before the sovereign debt turmoil that started in 2009), Portugal, Guatemala, Uruguay and Belgium.

184. See, for instance, J.W. Stigler, S. Smith & L.W. Mao (1985). The self-perception of competence by Chinese children. *Child Development, 56,* 1259–1270.

185. See, for instance, a very good discussion of self-efficacy in R. M. Klassen (2004) Optimism and realism: A review of self-efficacy from a cross-cultural perspective. *International Journal of Psychology, 39 (3),* 205–230.

186. Professor of Psychology Roy Baumeister cites the first two of these (the third is arguably more implicitly described in his book: R. F. Baumeister & J. Tierney (2012) *Willpower: discovering our greatest strength.* London: Allen Lane. How-ever, he's not talking about Courage when he cites them: he's talking about something that most people consider quite different – something I believe lies at the heart of courage. But we'll come to that in the next chapter.

187. In early drafts of this chapter, I called this the "I've earned it" effect. More recently, I came across the more compelling term "licence to sin", cited in K. McGonigal (2012) *Maximum Willpower: how to master the new science of self-control.* London: Macmillan. Again, the author is focused on willpower, rather than courage. Interestingly, she too refers to the "what the hell" effect, which I'd already incorporated thanks in part to Baumeister's influence, but which McGonigal clarified for me was first discovered by J. Polivy & C.P. Herman (2002) If At First You Don't succeed: False hopes of self-change. *American Psychologist, 52,* 677-689.

188. J. Haidt (2000). The positive emotion of elevation. *Prevention and Treatment, 3(3),* online edition.

189. From a Yale University study in which the individual in question was an actor, briefed to respond in a certain way: S. Barsade (2002) The ripple effect: emotional contagion and its influence on group behaviour. *Administrative Science Quarterly, 27,* 644-75 – cited in Goleman (2006) *op. cit.*

190. From page 123 of Badaracco, Jr. (2002) *op. cit.*

191. Ware (2012) *op. cit.*

192. I've not been able to find a source for this saying. 'Anonymous' is the closest I've managed to get.

193. P. G. Zimbardo (2006) The banality of evil, the banality of heroism. In J. Brockman (ed) *What is your dangerous idea?* p282-3. London: Simon & Schuster.

194. The term and some of the factors themselves, which we've already encountered elsewhere, appear in Zimbardo (2006) *op. cit.*

195. C.L.S. Pury (2008) Can Courage Be Learned? In S.J. Lopez (Ed.) *Positive Psychology: Exploring the best in people: Volume 1. Discovering human strengths*, 109-130. Westport, CT: Praeger. Cited in Biswas-Diener (2012) *op. cit.*

196. M. Cansdale (2012) *Developing Leaders: A Sandhurst guide (Pilot version).* The Royal Military Academy, Sandhurst.

197. D. Kahneman (2012) *Thinking Fast and Slow.* London: Penguin.

198. It's worth noting that Kahneman himself is keen to assert in his own book that "Systems 1 and 2 are not systems in the standard sense of entities with interacting aspects or parts. And there is no one part of the brain that either of the systems would call home." Kahneman (2012) *op. cit.*, p 29.

199. McGonigal (2012) *op. cit.*

200. People with well-developed emotion-regulation skills produced up to three times the number of antibodies in their immune system than people who didn't. See, for instance, M.A. Rosenkranz, D.C. Jackson, K.M. Dalton, I. Dolsrki, C.D. Ryff, B.H. Singer, D. Muller, N.H. Kalin & R.J. Davidson (2003) Affective style and in vivo immune response: neurobehavioral mechanisms. *Proceedings of the National Academy of Sciences, 100 (19)*, 11148-52.

201. Peter shared the basics of technique when we were working at Oxford-Saïd Business School in 2009. I've adapted it using techniques from NLP. Peter's provided a range of related techniques in P. Grünewald (2007) *The Quiet Heart: Putting stress in its place.* Edinburgh: Floris.

202. Some people say you should hold your breath for a count of five between inhaling and exhaling. I don't, because I believe it risks increasing the tension – but I can't say that belief is based on any hard scientific evidence.

203. Professor Xinyue Zhou at Sun Yat-sen University in China led this series of studies, which you can read in further detail in X. Zhou, T. Wildschut,C. Sedikides, X. Chen & A. Vingerhoets (2012). Heartwarming memories: nostalgia maintains physiological comfort. *Emotion* (electronically published ahead of print, and available at http://dx.doi.org/10.1037/a0027236)

204. J. Evans (2012) The Greeks' guide to living well. *The Times*, 8 May.

205. Based on two empirically-supported predictors of bravery, cited in Peterson & Seligman (2004) *op. cit.*

206. Michael Pritchard (a.k.a. Mike Dirnt) plays bass and provides backing vocals in American punk rock band Green Day.

207. This and 'accepting that we don't know everything' are two of four 'guiding principles of quiet leadership' extolled in Badaracco, Jr. (2002) *op. cit.*

208. In support of my distinction between ways of reducing the fear and ways to do it anyway, psychologists have found that (while it helps reduce our fear), practising emotional control does not strengthen our willpower. This observation is based on experiments using a range of strategies to try to increase self-control by managing one's emotions. See, for instance, M. Muraven, R.F. Baumeister & D.M. Tice (1999) Longitudinal improvement of self-regulation through practice: building self-control through repeated exercise. *Journal of Social Psychology, 139,* 446-57.

209. From page 83 of the first edition (undated) of *Serve to lead (An anthology).* Sandhurst, UK: The Royal Military Academy.

210. These findings are relatively recent. Some psychologists refer to 'ego depletion', others to 'willpower'. In my opinion, the most accessible book on the topic is Baumeister & Tierney (2012) *op. cit.*

211. B.J. Schmeichel, K.D. Vohs & R.F. Baumeister (2003) Intellectual performance and ego depletion: role of the self in logical reasoning and other information processing. *Journal of Personality and Social Psychology, 85,* 33-46.

212. Participants in one study chose between a $100 cheque that they could cash the same day and a $150 cheque that couldn't be cashed until a month after the experiment. X.T. Wang and R.D. Dvorak (2010) Sweet future: fluctuating blood glucose levels affect future discounting. *Psychological Science, 21,* 183-88.

213. The data to support this are referenced in Baumeister & Tierney (2012) *op. cit.* Studies include M. Oaten and K. Cheng (2006) Improved Self-Control: The benefits of a regular programme of academic study. *Basic and Applied Social Psychology, 28,* 1-16; M. Oaten and K. Cheng (2006) Longitudinal Gains In Self-Regulation From regular Physical Exercise. *British Journal of Health Psychology, 11,* 717-733; and M. Oaten and K. Cheng (2006) Improvements In Self-Control From Financial Monitoring. *Journal of Economic Psychology, 28,* 487-501.

214. Baumeister & Tierney (2012) *op. cit.*

215. Harris Interactive (2010) *Americans Report Willpower And Stress As Key Obstacles To Meeting Health-Related Resolutions.* American Psychological Association. This was a national survey, conducted in the US between February and April 2010, which is cited in McGonigal (2012) *op. cit.*

216. Also suggested in Baumeister & Tierney (2012) *op. cit.*

217. See, for instance, J.F. Thayer, A.L. Hansen, E. Saus-Rose & B.H. Johnsen (2009) Heart Rate Variability, Prefrontal Neural Function, And Cognitive Performance: The neurovisceral integration perspective on self-regulation, adaptation, and health. *Annals of Behavioral Medicine, 37,* 141-153 Cited in McGonigal (2012) *op. cit.*

218. J.J. Ratey (2008) *Spark! The revolutionary new science of exercise and the brain.* London: Little, Brown and Company.

219. A series of studies have shown this – M.T. Gaillot, R.F. Baumeister, C.N. DeWall et al (2007) Self-Control Relies On Glucose As A Limited Energy Source: willpower is more than a metaphor. *Journal of Personality and Social Psychology, 92,* 325-336.

220. S. Danziger, J. Levav & L. Avnaim-Pesso (2011). Extraneous factors in judicial decision. *Proceedings of the National Academy of Sciences, 108,* 6889-6892.

221. M. Hagger & N. Chatzisarantis (2012). The Sweet Taste of Success: The presence of glucose in the oral cavity moderates the depletion of self-control resources. *Personality and Social Psychology Bulletin, 39(1),* 28-42; and M.A. Sanders, S.D. Shirk, C.J. Burgin & L.L. Martin. (2012). The Gargle Effect: Rinsing the mouth with glucose enhances self-control. *Psychological Science, 23,* 1470-1472

222. From research by Charles Czeisler, Professor of Sleep Medicine at Harvard Medical School, discussed in B. Fryer (2006) Sleep deficit: the performance killer. A Conversation with Charles A. Czeisler. *Harvard Business Review, October.* (Retrieved from http://hbr.org/2006/10/sleep-deficit-the-performance-killeron 21 May 2012). I've been aware of the research for some time, but was directed to this particular piece by Heffernan (2012) *op. cit.*

223. OECD (2011) *Society at a Glance 2011 – OECD Social Indicators* (Retrieved from www.oecd.org/els/social/indicators/SAG on 20 July 2012). The majority of the data in this survey is from 2006, drawing on representative surveys of 18 countries, sampling between 4000 and 200,000 people per nation. The paper reported that the average person in most countries was getting at least eight hours a night. The French got the most, then Americans, and Japanese and Koreans got the least, but even they were close to eight hours.

224. A smaller scale study in the USA (of 669 people) showed that people consistently over-estimate the amount of sleep they get. Although the average person in the study said they slept 7½ hours a night, they spent only 6.1 hours asleep. University of Chicago Medical Center (2006) New Study Shows People Sleep Even Less Than They Think. *ScienceDaily,* 3 Jul Retrieved July 20, 2012, from

www.sciencedaily.com/releases/2006/07/060703162945.htm.

225. These questions come from p87 of George (with Sims) (2007) *op. cit.*

226. Mulcahy was CEO from August 2001 to July 2009. Much of her story as told here, and the quote, come from page 171 of George (with Sims) (2007) *op. cit.*

227. Mulcahy was awarded 'CEO of the Year' in 2008 by Chief Executive magazine (Retrieved from http://chiefexecutive.net/full-list-of-previous-ceo-of-the-year-award-winners on 5 May 2012). Sure, when she stepped down in 2009, the company's share price was in a less-than-desirable place. However, that doesn't detract from the Courage she showed prior to that.

228. M. Muraven & E. Slessareva (2003) Mechanisms Of Self-control Failure: Motivation and limited resources. *Personality and Social Psychology Bulletin, 29,* 894-906. Cited McGonigal (2012) *op. cit.*

229. See www.bp.com/sectiongenericarticle.do?categoryId=9039294&contentId= 7072267 (Retrieved 5 August 2013).

230. See the company's 2009 Sustainability Review at http://www.bp.com/content/ dam/bp/pdf/sustainability/country-reports/bp_sustainability_review_2009.pdf (Retrieved 5 August 2013).

231. National Commission on the BP Deepwater Horizon Oil Spill and Offshore Drilling (2011) *Deep Water: The Gulf Oil Disaster and the Future of Offshore Drilling.* Report to US President Obama. (Retrieved from www.oilspillcommission.gov/ final-report on 21 May 2012). See also The Bureau Of Ocean Energy Management, Regulation And Enforcement (2011). *Report Regarding The Causes Of The April 20, 2010 Macondo Well Blowout.* 14 September 14. (Retrieved from http://docs. lib.noaa.gov/noaa_documents/DWH_IR/reports/dwhfinal.pdf on 5 August 2013). If you're interested in the finer details of BP's culture, including their use of the children's tale *The Three Little Pigs* as a metaphor for valuing the lives of the people who subsequently died in the Gulf of Mexico, I'd strongly recommend you read Heffernan's book – Heffernan (2012) *op. cit.* It's also worth bearing in mind the role of "creeping determinism" in case studies like these. Often, people come out afterwards and say that they knew such an event was likely. Some are after the glory and publicity; others are simply subject to a common flaw with memory: in retrospect, they remember themselves being far more certain of the outcome than they actually were at the time. Malcolm Gladwell cites creeping determinism in claims that 9/11 should have been averted because the clues that those particular attacks were imminent were there in the files of the FBI, CIA and NSC. See M. Gladwell (2009) *What The Dog Saw.* London: Penguin. However,

Senator Richard Selby (vice chair of the Senate Select Committee on Intelligence that reported on September 11th) pointed out in his report that the FBI's counter-terrorism division alone has 68,000 outstanding and unassigned leads dating back to 1995, no more than 100 or so of which are likely to prove useful.

232. From page 75 of B. Franklin (1909) The Autobiography of Benjamin Franklin. New York: P.F. Collier & Son (Originally published in 1793). Cited in Baumeister & Tierney (2012) *op. cit.*

233. A number of studies are cited Baumeister & Tierney (2012) *op. cit.* They include R.A. Emmons & L.A. King (1988) Conflict Among Personal Strivings: Immediate and long-term implications for psychological and physical well-being. *Journal of Personality and Social Psychology, 54,* 1040-1048; and H.W. Maphet & A.L. Miller (1982) Compliance, Temptation, And Conflicting Instructions. *Journal of Personality and Social Psychology, 42,* 137-144.

234. See page 169 of Badaracco, Jr. (2002) *op. cit.*

235. *Ibid.* p127.

236. Information on E. Hamilton Lee retrieved from www.airmailpioneers.org/profiles/profile1.html on 24 July 2012.

237. Heifetz, Grashow & Linsky (2009) *op. cit.*

238. A definition of sustaining paradox that emerged from a conversation with Jane Boston and was more her work than mine.

239. D.H. Pink (2011) *Drive: The surprising truth about what motivates us.* Edinburgh: Canongate Books.

240. John Donahoe on page 3 of George (with Sims) (2007) *op. cit.*

241. From page xxxii of W. Bennis (1989) *On Becoming A Leader.* Boston, MA: Addison-Wesley.

242. Polivy & Herman (2002) *op. cit.*

243. From page xxv of George (with Sims) (2007) *op. cit.*

244. I first came across the concept of terminal and instrumental values in the work of Milton Rokeach – see, for instance M. Rokeach (1968) *Beliefs, attitudes, and values: a theory of organization and change.* San Francisco: Jossey-Bass; M. Rokeach (1973) *The nature of human values.* New York: Free Press.

• ● •

Lightning Source UK Ltd.
Milton Keynes UK
UKOW06f0206260917
309876UK00009B/47/P